Always Be Job Hunting

Lessons You Can Learn From Someone Who Has Landed
18 Jobs In 36 Years...And Never Stops Looking.

By

John N. Frank

With a contribution from Lynn Hazan

Cover Design by Jenny Frank

ISBN: 1475099045
ISBN 13: 9781475099041

Table of Contents

Chapter 1

Is There A Perfect Job?

This chapter talks about a job I started in June, 2010.

I just started a new job. Again. Landing a new job in the midst of the worst recession in my lifetime should be a reason for rejoicing, right? After all, U.S. unemployment has edged close to 10% and, according to recent studies, more than half the country's workers have either been laid off, taken a pay cut or are working in jobs way below their skill level (under-employed in the jobs-world vernacular).

So why am I not rejoicing over my good fortune? Well, part of it may be because to get a new job, I gave up a lot. I'm in that unlucky 50% who are under-employed. To find a new job after surviving for two years in an almost unbearable workplace, I agreed to take a pay cut of more than 20%. But it's not just the money; money has never been a chief motivator for me. I'm going to have to make adjustments because of the pay cut, of course, adjustments like contributing a lot less to my retirement savings, for example. But there's something more than money that I've given up and it bothers me. What?

You see, my new job is the 17th I've had in the 34 years since I got out of school. That works out to a new job every two years for my entire working life, although the average is a bit misleading since I worked for as little as one month at one job.

What I still think of as my worst job – although my last one is now competing for that title – was a place I stayed for exactly one year and 10 days. I disliked the workplace so much that I counted each day, just like someone in prison would do.

The job I just left lasted just shy of two years. I started in July of 2008, as the Great Recession started doing its worst to the economy, and left in June of 2010 as I and the rest of the country hoped things were improving, even as the stock market was predicting more troubles ahead for all of us.

My parents' generation (yes, I'm a Baby Boomer, born in 1953) worked with the hope, even sometimes the certainty, of lifetime employment at one company. That idea already was fading when I got out of school and it seems a distant memory today. Indeed, a *Bloomberg BusinessWeek* magazine's cover story a few years ago noted that everyone in the professional world will eventually just work as consultants and temporary workers.

Is my job changing simply a different definition of consulting or contract work? I think so. Switching employers every two years, which was once seen as the kiss-of-death for a career, is now somewhat normal. I'm not so much a harbinger of what's to come as I am the new norm. So why this book? Because since I've already tackled this rapid job hunting and changing employers – in fact, actively sought it out – I think others can benefit from my story. My employment history, my job-decision-making record, all contain lessons – from what to do to what to avoid – that you can use to keep yourself gainfully employed in today's uncertain world.

That's why I've set out to write this book. It's also why I've asked an executive search professional to comment on and critique my early job hunting. I've done a good job of finding work in hard times, of staying one step ahead of companies being shut down, sold or reorganized (all common occurrences in today's workplace and in my work history). I'm very proud of the fact that in my 34 years of working, I've only been unemployed for roughly a month and half – and this came early in my career, when the newspaper group where I worked was sold.

My goal is to give you a handbook you can use in your career and in your job-hunting quest. Learn from my mistakes and my triumphs – and learn from the pro's advice. Know through it all that you are a valuable human being who has a great deal to contribute to the workplace; temporary employment setbacks don't change that fact.

If you're honest about your capabilities, if you keep current with the ever-changing skills needed in your profession, and if you stay open to new possibilities, I think you will succeed more than you will fail.

So with all that said, what about this new job I have? I've recently agreed to become editorial director of two trade magazines related to the food business. They're based in suburban Chicago and were once part of a magazine group where I worked from 1993 through the end of 1995.

The magazines' ownership changed three times since I left. The founding owner of the company ran into financial difficulties while I was employed there in late 1995; indeed that's what prompted me to leave. How bad was it? The owner sold the magazine I was editing in order to raise more capital for his company. The prospective new owner wanted to cut my pay 30 percent and so I found a new job. Ironically, the sale fell through after I'd moved on. Then, the entire company was subsequently sold. In the end, the original owner got the new owners to keep him and his three sons, all of whom worked there, to manage the group. He even somehow managed to pull this off a second time when the group was sold yet again. The third time the group was sold, in 2007, he finally met owners who didn't want him around. He left – only to start a competing group of magazines, buying some food magazines put up for sale after most magazines saw their advertising income tank in the Great Recession.

Confused? Welcome to the world of magazine publishing. Like so many other 21st century American businesses, publishing is being ripped apart by the massive economic changes the Internet has caused. Advertisers now have much more effective, and much cheaper, ways of reaching their customers than most print magazines can provide. As a professional journalist, I worry more about what to write for magazines than I do about how they make money. But as an editorial manager for the latter part of my career, how magazines make money has impacted how I work and how much I can earn, so I'm acutely aware of magazine economics.

I know my current owners bought the group at the top of the market and are carrying a big debt load at the worst possible time. I also know they asked their employees to take 25 percent pay cuts to get through the recession. This request prompted people to leave, which is why there was an opening for me.

So in one sense, I feel like my career is going backwards to a place where I previously worked. This time around I'm overseeing two magazines instead of one. But I'm still concerned; Is it a good idea to go back to a previous employer?

This is actually the second time I've done this. The first time around, ownership had also changed and I really enjoyed working again with people I knew and respected as journalists. Today, I'll again work with old friends and colleagues, people I've worked with previously so there's some comfort in that. I also hit it off with the publisher who oversees my magazine, another positive. A trade magazine publisher is usually the chief ad salesperson for that magazine. In my latest case, he joined the company about a month before I did so he's bringing in new ideas and, I hope, a more positive way to get advertisers to work with us. We agree completely that today's magazines need to be multimedia endeavors that include e-newsletters, podcasts, webinars and anything else online that advertisers want to use to reach their customers.

My last boss didn't get that at all; she had no background in publishing and fired the publisher who hired me, thinking so little of his role that she didn't see the need to replace him. That organization, a trade association which also published magazines for its members, kept its Web site completely separate from its print publications. As a result, it basically wrote the death warrant for its print efforts. After two years of trying to convince my boss that we were missing the best way to keep making money from publishing, I gave up and accepted my new job.

My new publisher seems to get it and working with a boss who agrees with me and values my input is incredibly refreshing and exhilarating for me. I left my last job like a soldier who had fought one too many battles, and still had bad dreams about arguing with someone who had no respect for me as a journalist.

So, with a seemingly great new boss, why don't I feel better? Well for one, because he is new at this company, I keep wondering how much he'll actually be able to accomplish. Will the company's owners, who say they know they need changes to reinvigorate their magazines, actually allow him to shake up the old corporate culture? And what happens if he finds he can't do what he wants and he decides to leave? It wouldn't be the first time I've had a superior who threw in the towel and exposed me directly to intransigent senior management.

I've learned over the years that I need a buffer between me and the senior-most levels of corporate management. I tend to say what's on my mind when asked. Couching my thoughts in corporate speak has never been something I wanted to do or could do. I'm a journalist, after all, my whole being is trained to tell things as directly and as factually as I can. Delivering bad news is what I do for a living, hiding it is not something I enjoy.

So if my new publisher decides to leave, or doesn't meet his revenue targets and gets kicked out anytime soon, I may be back to where I was in terms of working with superiors I don't get along with.

The second reason I'm uneasy is because I miss my former editorial team at my last position and I really haven't spent enough time with my new team to know if we'll mesh nearly as well. I consider myself an excellent team builder who can bring out the best in people who work with me. In my last job, there were two people on staff when I arrived who were just coming into their professional primes as journalists and so they made my job incredibly easy. My managing editor and I often found ourselves completing each others sentences about issue planning, story ideas, what we thought of key industry issues. That type of symbiosis is so rare to find, I really had to think long and hard about leaving it behind (she subsequently left for a new job about a month after I did, so, even there, we were on the same page).

My new managing editor (a number two position in magazine publishing, normally just below the editor-in-chief) and I don't seem to have that same type of connection. I'm readjusting, brushing off my team-building skills, and trying to adapt to this new team. I also need to hire someone new for another position.

All of that is a long way of saying I miss my old staff. As a middle manager, it's difficult enough finding a boss you can mesh with; finding a team you lead that is in sync is hard too. Did I make a mistake by trading a bad boss for a good one while leaving a great team for an untested and much less experienced one?

And what about money? I've reached a salary plateau in my field. While I got a sizable raise in my last job to oversee four magazines, I was more than earning it by basically doing what had been two people's jobs there and later having a third added on top of that when the publisher was fired and I took responsibility for budgeting, negotiating with printers and other business functions.

My salary hasn't really changed much in the last 15 years, varying up and down maybe $20,000. So I plateaued, salary-wise, when I was 43 (I'm 58 as

I write this). That is more than depressing. Has it been my job choices that led me here or is the U.S. economy just that stagnant? It's no secret that what was once called the industrial economy has been falling apart since the 1970s when I got out of college. Now even the post-industrial economy – services, information and technology – seems to be fleeing U.S. shores. Am I just a symbol of reduced American earning power?

The last thing that has me a bit worried is that I had actually reached out to that former owner of these magazines I mentioned earlier to ask him his thoughts. He had nothing but negative things to say about my new employer, as might be expected, given that they didn't want to keep him or his sons around after their purchase.

But he's doing more than just talking; he's started a new publishing venture of his own and has just started a magazine that will compete directly with the main magazine I'm overseeing. He hired away the editor I replaced, the former managing editor and the old publisher and associate publisher to staff his new magazine, which means he starts with an experienced staff with widespread industry contacts. There's no doubt that what he wants to do is drive us out of business, or at least get the company to the point where it would sell him my magazine so he could combine the two into one.

This could result in my being out of work again. I suppose this is my most far-fetched worry but I've been through things like it before so it hangs over me as well.

So for this chapter, I asked executive search veteran Lynn Hazan, president of Chicago-based search firm Lynn Hazan & Associates, (http://www. lhazan.com) did I make a good career decision in taking this new job? What can others learn, right and wrong, from what I've done? Are my fears justified? And how about the way I went about getting this job? I networked like crazy, adding LinkedIn connects until I'm over 300 now, for example. Yet this job came from a simple want ad on a journalism job site. I sent in a resume and a cover letter emphasizing my food writing experience and my prior experience with this very group of magazines, and that seemed to get me in the door. Yet everything I read says ads are the wrong way to find a job today, what's the right way?

Lynn Hazan Advises:

First of all John, congratulations on being able to land a wonderful new opportunity, in spite of a down market. That says so much about your credentials and professionalism. You have a lot to contribute to your new company.

Here are some thoughts based on my 26 years in the recruiting business.

First, the rules have changed. Career paths that candidates followed in the past aren't necessarily the ones that are going to lead them into the future. Our clients' needs for staffing have also changed. Given the complexities of the job market and the fact that there are so many people looking for work, one of the most important things a candidate can do is to be flexible. Hiring managers and candidates need to think both short and long-term. With fewer full-time positions that need to be filled, our clients are increasingly requesting freelance talent. This isn't entirely bad news; often a part-time job can become full-time and candidates have opportunities to showcase their worth and create demand for their talent.

The fact that you took a pay cut, however painful that might be, is also a reflection of the new reality. Many companies need to do more with less. They've lost income and have less money in their budgets to pay their employees.

However, as we've all learned, money isn't everything. The recession has definitely taught us the importance of being thrifty and learning to determine, and sometimes re-determine, our priorities.

For example, many people have cut back on restaurant dining experiences. In the process they have re-discovered the art of cooking and re-established home as a safe haven. Families are now eating together more often and appreciate good food and conversation at home. I am a huge fan of home cooking and love to prepare my own cuisine, especially using organic vegetables from a CSA (community supported agriculture) farm. These are a few of the benefits that have come out of this recession.

Holding 17 jobs in 34 years is probably a record in my book. The fact that you've only been unemployed for a month and a half in your entire career speaks accolades about you and what you've contributed to employers.

You've been a builder. You've consistently expanded your knowledge and learned new tools, technologies and industries. This allowed you to become a subject matter expert. Clearly you have created demand for your talent.

The fact that you applied for this new job, again speaks about your abilities to learn, grow and to keep yourself competitive. Today's candidate need to be nimble. Job hunting is like riding a wave. Let's take the analogy of a wave. I view the recruiting business in a very similar way. You want to get on the wave as it builds momentum and ride it. You either want to get off before it peaks or get on to the next emerging wave. You must cultivate foresight and a sense of what's to come. You must also be able to adapt quickly to changing circumstances. This isn't always easy. In today's job market, candidates need to literally reinvent themselves and continually create demand for their expertise and talent.

As for how you found your job, there's no one size fits all model. John, you discovered this new job through an industry vertical website. These are actually very good sources. These portals reach professionals in specific verticals. You did your research and took command of your own destiny versus waiting for a potential hiring manager to find you.

Hiring patterns have changed dramatically over the last few years. Fortune 500 companies aren't hiring. They've trimmed staff and budgets, are sitting on assets and aren't spending money on growth. Job growth and opportunities tends to come from smaller entrepreneurial companies, or niche players. These companies have a chance to grow and succeed without having too many layers or complex bureaucracies.

You raise interesting points about returning to work for a former employer. There are many reasons candidates leave their employers to pursue other jobs and career paths. Often, it's because the next step doesn't exist or didn't exist at that time. Candidates may also feel the need to leave in order to be competitive and to grow professionally.

It's important to note that many companies have alumni associations, much like colleges and universities. This is particularly evident in professional services companies. They encourage their former employees to return as clients or future employees, and to use their services again. Business and relationships come back 360-degrees. If candidates leave on good terms from their employers and don't burn bridges, they can be seen as assets when they return. Isn't it a wonderful feeling to know that you can come home? Home may have changed from the original experience that compelled you to leave. Now, a new and different opportunity exists when a candidate returns.

If you look at the Gallup organization, they use a fascinating process to determine successful hires and long-term engagement. The Gallup organization notes that factors that point to successful hires and their long-term engagement with a company include if the employee has a "best friend at work." John, the fact that you've had very good friends at your jobs has been a real asset for you. It is one of the chief reasons that you've been happy to go to work everyday. That is a very important aspect, to have good collegial relationships. Now that you are supervising a larger staff you can draw from your previous experiences as both a colleague and a supervisor. You can groom your staff and help it realize that work can provide a wonderful social opportunity, as long as we get our jobs done. The relationships and culture that we build at work extend into the interpersonal. The ability to have good collegial relationships is something that you have experienced, and hopefully now you can model for your staff.

Where are the growth opportunities? Throughout your career changes, you've demonstrated your willingness and flexibility to continue learning. For example, gaining an understanding of agriculture and the commodities markets has served you well. You've become a subject matter expert and have been sought after as a professional. We all need to reinvent ourselves, along with our subject matter expertise, as it changes over time. The more we can prove that we're relevant, the less likely we are to lose our jobs.

Today's clients will only hire if there is a need for new staff due to growth, opportunity, and/or to replacement of an existing position. Each company has its challenges and opportunities. Your experience and success at so many different companies means you can now be recognized as a problem solver or the "fix it" man. This is another avenue for you to create demand for your talent.

You raise interesting issues about being compensated as a journalist. Sadly, journalism salaries aren't competitive with those in corporate or agency sectors. When journalists start in the profession they are often idealistic, eager to work hard and willing to accept lower compensation. As they progress within the field, they discover that salaries are not competitive. It is also difficult for candidates to increase their earnings. The jobs cap out in salary bands. Often the only way to raise compensation is to leave the company or move to a larger market. Unfortunately, journalism reflects an antiquated business model as it relies heavily on advertising revenue in order to raise enough money for salaries. John, as you can see from your own experience, this profession hasn't kept up with new models of compensation for employees. Hopefully new models will emerge, providing benchmarks to learn from.

What does it mean to be a journalist in the 21st century? Journalism jobseekers must re-examine if they want to continue working as professional journalists, or use journalism as a stepping-stones to different career opportunities. Journalists can apply their skill sets to corporate communications, marketing communications and new fields within social media. There are new opportunities and even new professions that didn't exist five years ago, like that of social media manager. Now whole departments are dedicated to these areas and professional communicators can make huge contributions.

If a journalism candidate wants to change jobs, it's good to ask: "where do I want to be in five years;

what should I be earning; is the journalistic route the one to pursue? Candidates should pursue their passion for journalism with eyes wide open. Finances definitely have a role to play. You must question working in a profession that systematically under-pays its workers. Are there other pluses that you can gain from your work? Are there other models for employment and compensation?

The whole notion of getting a job today has changed. John, I commend you on your ability to create social networks. You are using 21st century technology to help garner support, draw attention, source other resource people and position yourself as a leader.

One final thought. Finding a job today and be-ing hired requires more than pure writing ability. As George Harrison so aptly reminds us: "If you don't know where you're going, any road will take you there."

It's time to hire the right candidate, to get on the right bus, to go in the right direction. May you be our leader!

Chapter 2

Getting Your First Job

E ven after 36 years in the work world (two years have passed since I took the job mentioned in Chapter 1), I clearly remember what it was like to look for my first job. I remember like it was yesterday because, as a journalist, remembering things is what I do for a living. And because I have been filing away job-hunting lessons ever since. In a very really way, I have become a professional job hunter, which is why I'm writing this book, to share the fruits of my learning with you.

Back in 1975, I was job hunting in the midst of a horrible economy, just as so many, including my own children, are doing today.

While job-search technology has dramatically changed in the nearly four decades since, you can still learn lessons from what I did. Combine the lessons with today's tools and, hopefully, you'll land that first – and next – job.

I graduated from Marquette University in spring, 1975, a time when the country also was reeling from a recession. Despite getting a few interviews, the possibility of finding a full-time job seemed dim. Besides the economy, I also had to deal with some stiff competition in a popular field. My hoped-for profession, journalism, was flooded with people like me who wanted to change the world. The book and hit movie, "All the President's Men,' which detailed how two until-then obscure beat reporters at the *Washington Post* essentially toppled a power-hungry president, sent students flooding into journalism school. I graduated with thousands of others who all wanted to become the next Woodwards and Bernsteins. I even had a double major in journalism and political science specifically to become a political reporter, the very specialty it seemed everyone else was pursuing.

That's me, second from the left, with friends and classmates as we prepared to graduate from Marquette University in 1975.

To make matters worse, newspapers were dying—yes even then. Television was killing the afternoon paper, the publications people once depended on as the timeliest way to get breaking news. Only morning papers were making money and seemed likely to survive.

This all became clear during my interview at the *Milwaukee Journal* (which no longer exists) where the assistant managing editor laid out the state of my hoped-for profession and suggested I do something that I'd never thought of, go get a masters degree in journalism to set myself apart from the journalism graduate flood.

Journalism is hardly an academic profession. Once you learn the basics of writing and reporting, the best way to become better at both is to do them. As the editor of both my high school and college newspapers, I felt ready to report. But a lot of my peers had done and could say the same. The editor's advice made sense, especially if I could get a degree from a prestige journalism school; it might open some interview doors.

I was about to graduate from Marquette University in Milwaukee. While Marquette is well respected in its home state, there weren't many journalism jobs in Wisconsin. One company owned both newspapers and the city's major television station in Milwaukee, so if it didn't want to hire you, your choices were leave town or go work for the post office, which the editor of our student magazine actually did after graduation. My dad worked for the postal service at the time, so I decided one Frank there was enough. I wanted to be a journalist.

The big-name journalism school in the Midwest was Northwestern University in suburban Chicago. In the East, it was Columbia University in my native New York City. I applied to and interviewed at both but decided on Northwestern. I didn't want to go back home so early in my career. I needed to make my own way to prove I could do it. Northwestern offered me a scholarship, which eased the financial burden on my parents. So Northwestern it was.

But once I began my studies at Northwestern, I became a completely different kind of student than I'd been at Marquette. There, I'd been fixated on grades. Even now I can tell you my undergrad GPA (3.72 on a four-point scale). I had one C in four years of classes and that was in an advanced math elective I took because I liked math. Through my junior and into my senior years, I went three straight semesters with all As, while simultaneously working as managing editor of the school paper junior year and editor-in-chief senior year. That was highly unusual since an editor's grades usually drop precipitously because of all the work involved in producing the newspaper. My final semester, I took an independent study course and got only a B in Fiction Writing, which upset me mightily. For more than three decades I've shied away from writing fiction because of that B.

So you get the point: grades consumed me as an undergrad. But from the first day at Northwestern until the day I got a job offer just a few days before graduation, my job in grad school was finding a job. This most important of all lessons has stayed with me all these years, FINDING A JOB IS A JOB, don't ever think of it as anything less. A job search will be tough and frustrating, discouraging and disappointing, but it's a job that you must do well to achieve success.

In the 1970s, job hunting began with, first, typing your resume on a typewriter. Using a typewriter entailed taking a lot of time to ensure your resume didn't have typos, awkward phrases, or the wrong citations for anything you'd written or done. I give thanks daily for PCs and spell-check.

Once you completed a master resume, you made copies, lots of copies, and mailed them out along with cover letters. Today, companies use resume scanning software to find keywords that match what they're looking for. In the old days, you had to basically mind-read to figure out what an employer wanted.

Wording in want ads often was the best clue to what to emphasize, and this still holds true. Employers also are attracted by confident candidates so I often used the phrase "look no further" in my cover letters, as in "look no further for your next municipal reporter."

Hokey, yes, but I was amazed how many times during interviews that an editor mentioned that my using this phrase really made my resume stand out from the pile. For aspiring journalists, another key for job hunting was including samples of your work, what are known as clips, the actual stories that an editor liked enough to print. And yes, back in the day we clipped our stories out of newspapers, kept a master file and then copied them to send with resumes. Today, they go as PDF attachments.

Class assignments don't count as clips. I had clips from the *Marquette Tribune* but during my first quarter at Northwestern I built up my clip file with a vengeance. I took advantage of a program that sent students to Washington, D.C. for a quarter to report and write for various newspaper clients. The lesson? Search out and grab any chance to experience real-world employers evaluating and using your work. You'll be light years ahead of competing job seekers who can only talk about school projects.

My D.C. beat was the U.S. Department of Agriculture. I grew up in New York and knew little to nothing about agriculture but the program coordinators told me that going to college in Wisconsin led them to believe that I'd understood dairy farming and related Ag topics. I didn't complain and it worked out well. The Northwestern news service clients included many newspapers in strong agricultural states and they all wanted stories from Washington from their student intern. I gladly obliged and my stories ran in papers all over the farm belt of the Midwest, Upper Midwest and South. By December, a client newspaper in Freeport, IL which needed an Ag reporter, actually offered me a job. If I agreed to quit school and move to Freeport, the job was mine.

That paper dangling a real job was a real temptation. The job hunt would be over before it began. Yet, I decided against it. I wanted to finish my degree, a journalism masters only required one year and I was already a third of the way through it by then. I worried that if I were to quit and go to work, I'd possibly never go back and finish my degree.

Also, Freeport wasn't exactly my first choice of a place to live. It wasn't because it was a small town. To a New Yorker, every place is pretty much a small town. But I was dating another journalism student at the time and we'd agreed to look for work in places where we could both find jobs. That pretty much limited my search to cities in the Midwest where she was from and wanted to stay.

It can be extremely tough to turn down a job offer, especially in a tough economy. But if it doesn't seem right, it doesn't seem right. I still believe that today.

I returned to Northwestern in January 1976 with a complete shift in my student mentality. Grades no longer mattered to me. My potential employers wanted clips; grades weren't mentioned in my job interviews. Now this is not the case for many other careers, in fact there are many employers who'll ask recent grads for their grade point averages, so if you're still a student, please don't just stop working on getting good grades. The point is know what matters most to your potential employers and do what you can to make yourself more attractive.

So instead of spending my weekends writing and rewriting class assignments as I did in undergrad days, I scoured the want ads in every Midwest newspaper found in the library. In those days, job ads were printed in the Sunday papers so job hunting was a Sunday morning experience. Today, it obviously is 24/7 since ads are online and posted every day throughout the day. I'd advise you to sign up for daily job posting e-mails from job sites in the field you work in. These specialized sites are everywhere and can be a great place to begin your search.

My goal was to send out five job letters each week. With today's technology, I'd set that number a lot higher. My math background tells me you have to send out big numbers to get responses. I know people who say they've sent out 200 resumes looking for that first job without a response. My reaction is: "What's wrong with your resume?" If 200 people can look at it and not one potential employer is impressed enough to call, or a resume software program isn't picking up pertinent key words that the job entails, what have you forgotten to highlight about yourself?

I didn't just let my resume and cover letters speak for me. I also sent editors letters mentioning that I'd just happen to be in their particular city and asked if I could stop in just to introduce myself. This tactic required an investment – I took the $2,000 I had in the bank and bought a car, a Chevy Vega, to get me to those interviews. The Vega was one of Detroit's most famous lemons but it did the job for me. It took me from Peoria to points north like Fond du Lac, Wis. I'd often skip class and leave on Fridays for these trips. During spring break I drove all over the Midwest, meeting editors instead of going back to New York to visit my family.

On campus, Northwestern touted the fact that media executives came to campus to interview. Although most of these recruiters didn't have actual jobs to offer, I signed up for the interviewing practice and for any tips they could give me. Just meeting them validated my decision to go to a name grad school. The Northwestern degree on my resume rated. I wasn't as impressed with the grad school faculty compared to my professors at Marquette but I also had a completely different focus in grad school. What can I say? If there's a way to impress a potential employer in your field, use it.

So what did a five-month tour of Midwest papers get me? Lots of interviews but, with graduation only a few weeks away, no job offers. My decision to walk away from the Freeport paper was looking pretty stupid, especially since they no longer wanted to consider someone who'd once spurned them.

By May, jobs seemed to be the only topic classmates and I discussed. Some were holding out for offers from major newspapers or broadcast outlets. They were willing to find part-time jobs to make ends meet until they got their dream job. For me, any job was a dream job. When I read a notice from a string of suburban Chicago papers that needed a summer intern/reporter, I signed up to interview even though classmates said it would be a thankless job. My response? If they offered a paycheck, I would give thanks. I just hoped an internship would give me a chance to collect more clips and impress someone, somewhere enough to hire me full-time.

I arrived at the interview with my book of clips and a positive attitude and got the job. It was three days before graduation. My first day was the day after Northwestern graduation and I made sure to be the first reporter in the newsroom that morning. That decision paid off; a big story broke and the managing editor looked around, saw only me and sent me to cover the story. I ended up on the front page for three days in a row.

Within three weeks, I was offered a full-time job. My intern salary was $170 a week. With the full-time offer, I got a raise to $175 a week. Oh, but everything was cheaper then so that was enough money, you may think. Not really. My rent was $250 a month, I was facing 10 years of paying off college loans *and* I was about to get married. Should I have held out for a higher-paying job? I doubt it would've come along. Your first job is about getting experience, not getting rich, unless you're an attorney or in some other profession that pays new grads big bucks.

Little could I have imagined what jobs, or how many jobs, would follow that first one. My plan then was to stay there for up to five years and then move to a bigger newspaper. That wasn't exactly what happened.

Lessons for You:

- ✓ Build up real-world experience before graduation.

- ✓ There are no bad first jobs, if you can gain experience that you use to find future positions.

- ✓ Job Hunting is a Job.

Chapter 3

Landing My First Management Job

Once I had my first newspaper job, I did almost everything and anything that was asked of me to develop as broad a portfolio of skills and experience as I could. A first job is a time to learn about your chosen profession, I believe, and to develop a wide range of abilities so you can move up the ladder in your field. If you only learn to do one thing, you won't be prepared for a new job or a new employer should your current one decide you're expandable at some point.

My full-time job was education reporter, covering three local school boards and two community colleges. This meant I worked from 2 p.m. until whenever three or four nights a week. School board meetings normally started at 7 p.m. and with contentious issues on the agenda, could go well past midnight. I took notes during the meetings, then raced to a pay phone (no cell phones in those days) to call in a story that I was writing in my head, even as I dictated it to someone on the newsroom's copy desk back in the office.

I know this routine sounds like it's out of a movie and you may be wondering, "How can someone write while they're talking?" but that's exactly what I learned to do. I loved it. Thinking really fast on my feet is something I still enjoy. Mastering this skill came in handy years later when in the early 1980s I worked for Reuters, the international wire service, covering the collapse of a major Midwest bank.

In addition to meeting coverage, I wrote budget stories, myriad human interest pieces about teachers, especially those who seemed to really connect with their students, and school programs. Title IX, a federal law that requires schools to offer girls the same athletic options as boys, had just been enacted, so I wrote many stories covering the beginning of girls' sports programs at local schools and the community colleges. I also wrote about other big changes in education, including the efforts to mainstream children with learning disabilities into regular classrooms.

All that came under the heading of my main work at the paper, what's known as a reporter's beat. But since the paper was relatively small, all reporters also took turns on other assignments. I worked one Saturday each month, being on call for any breaking weekend news (the paper was a daily with a Saturday but no Sunday edition at the time, it would eventually publish seven days a week as the suburbs it served Northwest of Chicago grew tremendously in the late 1970s and early 1980s).

Saturday work included diverse assignments like covering fair housing marches in white Chicago neighborhoods that African-Americans were trying to integrate at the time, or rushing to O'Hare to meet a plane full of people who had been hijacked and then released by terrorists (passenger plane hijacking occurred with some regularity in those pre-9/11 days).

The paper's reporters could also write extra stories outside of our beats, like restaurant reviews, (we got free meals for our work), or features for the paper's Saturday magazine, for which we were paid freelance writing fees. Reporting and writing magazine stories not only brought in some extra income, it helped me develop a longer-form writing style.

The building where I had my first reporting job is gone now, only an empty lot is there. But the newspaper has survived in the Chicago suburb of Arlington Heights.

Most daily stories were short. Those stories I called in, for example, filled eight column inches of space, or about 500 words. Other stories might go to 1,000 words. Magazine stories ran in the 2,000-word range. Writing stories of varying lengths requires different techniques, approaches, and even different reporting methods. So the wider the variety of assignments I could get, the more skills I could develop.

I've spent the majority of my career in magazines, but I've written for wire services, web sites, blogs and newsletters. Being willing to tackle the variety of experiences I developed in that first job has, I think, allowed me the flexibility to work for any type of publication, including today's ever-evolving online work.

The lesson? Challenge yourself to do as much as possible in your first job – and in every job that follows – and fight against industry, management or even your own impulse to be pigeon-holed into one very narrow focus. In your first few jobs, your career is just beginning; experience it to the fullest; because you can never really know where it will all take you. In every job, even as you begin to specialize, try to take on new assignments and responsibilities; you never know where your new skills will take you.

I stayed on the education beat for about a year and a half but then a reporting spot opened up to cover a local town's government. Being a political reporter was what I had trained for in college and so I applied to transfer and got the new beat. I became the Buffalo Grove reporter (don't laugh; it's a suburb of Chicago, not a place you would image buffalo roaming, but at the time they were built, the name did give the tract homes a certain Western romance). Changing beats wasn't the norm then, but I wanted to experience it all and this seemed like an opportunity to get to work on the specialty I'd trained for.

Covering Buffalo Grove politics meant writing about lots of meetings. These included the village, its park district board, zoning board (a big deal in a town that was growing quickly and so approving lots of new housing developments), and its appearance control commission (the group that approved a developer's design plans before construction could begin). I became a fixture around town as I looked for stories. It was during my Buffalo Grove days that I ordered vanity license plates, JNF39, for my car (I still have those plates today, although now my daughter drives that car) so that people would know that I was at village hall or the park district office if they were looking for me with a story idea. This was in the days before cell phones, and it wasn't as easy to quickly find someone as it is today. I invested in those plates as a way to do my job better. I also kept writing stories that were not on my official job description, like my restaurant reviews and Saturday features.

After about a year I discovered that government reporting wasn't all I had expected it to be. I looked around our newsroom for another opportunity, a beat that hopefully would mean getting home by 6 p.m. instead of midnight three or four nights a week. I had married a year after starting my job. My wife was a reporter at the time too. She worked for another local newspaper and also had a night meeting schedule to deal with, so a new assignment that would have us home more together seemed like a good idea for the marriage as well. Balancing work schedules in a two-earner family is always a challenge. It's one I still wrestle with today as I am trying to make a second marriage work.

Luckily back then, our one business reporter (the group I worked for published more than a dozen suburban dailies at the time but had only one business reporter whose work ran in all of them) was leaving.

During college I'd spent my summers working as a messenger on Wall Street. My mother had worked for a mutual fund before I was born and my father had worked for an importing firm in the Wall Street area, so my family always had an interest in the stock market. A cousin found me the Wall Street summer job and I enjoyed learning about the markets. Indeed, while at Northwestern getting my masters, I took the available business writing courses to learn more about this world. (Again, I'm always trying to learn new subjects and skills.)

My Wall Street background and my business courses were enough to convince the managing editor that I could be the new business reporter (I actually applied to him with a letter outlining my credentials for the job, a more formal approach that no one else there took). At the time, business reporting was a journalism backwater. In the mid-1970s, most newspaper readers didn't think much about the economy or focus on Wall Street like they do today.

Luckily for me, that was all about to change. The country would soon be in the grip of hyper-inflation. Interest rates for mortgages climbed to 14-18 percent for a time, and readers suddenly cared a great deal about business, interest rates, and their savings. They also started caring about Wall Street and investing as mutual funds became a big part of America's financial life and company-run pension plans gave way to the new 401K plans that let employees decide where to invest their own retirement contributions.

I covered all those topics and many others. I interviewed the then CEO of United Airlines about how the company would cope with airline deregulation (not very well as it turned out, but that's a different book). I found I enjoyed business writing, which surprised me given my early interest in political writing. I'd always had an aptitude for math and it served me well in business writing. Most writers tend to be afraid of numbers, and believe they're either a word or a numbers person. I can be both, and I think more people could be if they ignore their own stereotypes, another job-hunting lesson.

I wrote so much about so many different business topics that I asked for a new job title. Even though I had no staff, I wanted to be called the business editor of the papers, not just business reporter. I thought the editor's title would reflect the amount of work I was doing. In addition to my own writing I also assembled a daily business page, editing wire service copy, selecting photos and trying to give a quick round-up of the day's business highlights. Several days a week, we ran more than one page of business news, so I was then putting together a business section, more responsibility than a reporter title implies. My managing editor refused. This upset me and I started looking for a new job. I'd been at paper about two and a half years.

So, was I too rash? Were my reasons for wanting the new title legitimate? Were they worth leaving this job? How long is too long at a first job? And how much rejection or disappointment should someone take at a job before looking elsewhere? I think it depends on your own ability to deal with job stress and with your own personal career goals.

Throughout my career, I've been quick, maybe too quick, to take offense and move on. I realized early on in my career that a major reason for this was seeing what working at an unpleasant job did to my father. When I was young, he'd worked for a food importing company. He'd started as a messenger and worked his way up to the executive level, a major accomplishment for someone who hadn't finished high school because, during the Great Depression to help his family, he'd quit school to find work.

He was always self-conscious about his lack of education and, as a result, never felt he fit in at his company. He was always tense and, I'm sure, took on the toughest, most thankless tasks to prove himself. The stress wore on him until the day the scarred-over stomach ulcers he'd developed during his World War II service in the Pacific burst open and he was rushed to the hospital for an operation to re-build his stomach. The surgery was high risk and the outcome uncertain; as my dad was being taken away an uncle told me that I might never see him again. I was 11 years old.

He survived, but left the hospital weighing less than 100 pounds and needed a year at home to recu-perate. Suspecting that the stress at the import firm was going to literally kill him, just before the ulcers erupted he'd started a new job with the post office. He spent the last 20 years or so of his working life in a low-stress mail handler job. He refused every promotion offered him and even worked nights to avoid higher stress day work.

Although I was only in fifth grade when he had his surgery, the experience marked me for life. I vowed that I'd never let a job become that stressful. My dad's experience and my promise to myself has prompted me at times to leave jobs after arguments with superiors or changes within the company. In some cases, this self-preservation instinct had kept me one step ahead of layoffs, so it's been good. But in one or two instances, I think I left too hastily. Specifically I had two jobs later in my career that I should never have left. You'll read more about them as you continue through the book. But as a brief overview, one I left because I didn't want to pay the price it required to stay there, namely transferring from city to city across the country and the world. The other I left after an angry e-mail outburst at a boss made me an outcast with the senior managers closest to him. That turned out to haunt me years later when he was running another publishing company and those same subordinates of his refused to consider me for any job because of my history (what I thought of as ancient history by then since it had happened more than a decade earlier) with him. Lesson to Learn: Don't burn your bridges lightly, and don't send out e-mails when you're angry.

Getting back to my first job, I was ready for an editor's title. While my peers thought of themselves primarily as reporters, I'd always thought of myself as an editor, a role I'd loved on my high school and college papers. An editor's job involves planning issues, working with staff to develop stories, editing the stories and creating a final product, a newspaper (or later in my career, a magazine or a Web site or e-newsletter). I believed my career destiny was to lead, to build and create rather than just report and write. I also wanted to lead a team, something that wasn't an option where I was. So I went back to job hunting.

Who would hire someone three years out of school as an editor? In those days, youth wasn't the selling point it is today, particularly in the tech field, where the younger you are, the better. My experience wasn't much experience at all in those days of grizzled old newsmen – and yes, almost all of them were men.

So I set my sights on smaller suburban Chicago newspaper chains that paid less than big city dailies but might be more open to hiring someone with less experience. My resume and cover letters played up the special projects and special reporting teams I'd overseen as business reporter. I came across a small chain of six suburban weekly newspapers still owned by the man who'd built the company, a wily old former Illinois state senator, whom everyone still called senator. He was turning the reins of operation over to his son, who wasn't much older than me. Fortunately for me, the son didn't get along with the current editor, fired him, and needed a new one.

Once again, colleagues told me I was crazy to go from a daily chain to weeklies, a step backwards in the journalism job hierarchy of the day. But I saw the job as a stepping-stone for management experience;

it was what I wanted. I took it, getting a raise to what then seemed like a princely sum of $15,000 a year, and prepared to start the management part of my career in January, 1979. Little did I know that the next year would include covering a mass murderer, being among the first on the scene of a major airline crash at O'Hare airport, and finding out what happens when your company – and your job – are sold out from under you. But that's the next chapter.

Lessons for You:

✓ Continuously work on new skills. Don't let anyone label you.

✓ Ask for the change you want. You just might get it.

✓ Understand why you want to change jobs and be realistic about the timing.

✓ Listen to other advice but own your own career goals. It's your work, your life.

Chapter 4

Learning On the Job

Looking back all these years later, I'm struck by the hubris with which I took my first management job. I really did think I knew it all and started out with that attitude, alienating people who'd been at their jobs there for decades by the time I'd arrived. I subsequently lived through working for new managers who did the same thing to me. I've wished they had listened to me by using the resources at hand rather than quickly dismissing the insights of people who'd been on the scene before they arrived.

I guess in some ways I've been paid back for the mistakes I made in that first management job. Life's funny when it does that to us isn't it?

Getting back to discussing that first management job, I started as the managing editor (a title my new boss let me pick) of six weekly north and northwest suburban Chicago newspapers in January, 1979 just after one of the biggest snow storms in the area's history. Another huge story was the recent arrest of mass murderer John Wayne Gacy, who was charged with the murders of 33 teenage boys and young men. He'd lured his victims to his home and buried most of them in the crawl space beneath his house – a house that was in Norwood Township, the circulation area of one of our newspapers. The Gacy case still remains one of the most gruesome in Illinois, and U.S., crime history.

I swept into my new job determined to cover the Gacy case better than any other newspaper in our area (a tall order for a case that received national attention). I also wanted to make a batch of other changes. First, I convinced Junior (the senator's son) that he should pay everyone more. The senator was a notorious penny pincher. For example, instead of buying paper for us to type our stories on (we used typewriters then and newsrooms normally were awash in paper), he insisted that we use the back of press releases that came into our offices. Today he might be called green, but in those days, he was just cheap. Indeed, I'd heard that being cheap was how he'd built his mini-newspaper empire and amassed a real estate empire that stretched all the way to South America.

The senator had paid editors about $120 a week, low even by the standards of the day. I convinced Junior to pay $140 a week and to expand the staff. We also went shopping for a new building. Our offices were in a small building that had once housed a small post office branch. It had seen better days, to say the least. Peeling paint barely covered the walls and the roof leaked every time it rained. We had one desk that became a lake because of that leak; the person who sat there had to move temporarily into another room during each storm.

With my plans to hire more reporters underway, we were in desperate need of space. My wife at the time described our newsroom as 12 desks inside a Volkswagen, which wasn't far from the truth. So Junior went shopping with the senator's money and bought a building around the block from us in suburban Park Ridge, a town to which Hillary Clinton would someday bring national fame. The new building had been home to a Woolworth's, a five and ten cents store chain that had once been a major force in American retailing but was already in its decline at that time.

I hired three recent Marquette graduates as new reporters. They'd all worked for me on the student newspaper and so I felt I knew them and needed their talents. I wanted people who could write quickly and write about a wide range of topics. I also wanted people with formal journalism training because so many of the staff Id inherited had learned their trade on their jobs.

You can imagine the existing staff's reaction to this influx of young guns. I'd created a divided work force. Finally after a few weeks of these changes, one of the veterans explained that while she could accept some of the changes I was proposing, that I needed to respect the input of veteran employees. I realized she was right. I held a staff meeting to air out concerns and to get us on a better footing. I paired up the new reporters with vets and asked the old timers to teach and the new folks to listen and learn. Most important, I started to listen and to explain my thought process instead of merely changing things.

While all these changes were enacted, the senator was out of the country, taking his latest wife on a honeymoon that included visits to his South American properties. Junior and I were free to spend and do as we pleased and, truly, we were like two kids in a candy shop.

All our spending stopped when the senator got back to town. He exploded, berating Junior for his spending ways. To make matters worse, shortly after Junior bought our new building its roof collapsed under the weight of all the snow from that monster storm I mentioned, leaving us with a building with, well, no roof.

I'd changed some of the senator's favorite sections of the newspapers, making pictures on the local society page smaller, for example. He told me to change the format back, which I did begrudgingly.

He also said we should stop writing about Gacy even though the story was still very much a part of Chicago media coverage months after he'd been arrested.

The victims' families had been through enough, he told me. I thought about it, and agreed. This wasn't a time to follow the journalism pack, it was a time to stand apart and recognize that people expected something entirely different from their local papers than they did from the big Chicago dailies or local television news. Community newspapers really were part of the communities they covered. In school I'd been taught to think of the story first and let consequences fall where they may. Journalism schools didn't really prepare their graduates for work at smaller suburban newspapers, yet that's where the jobs were at the time, that's where I was working and that's where I had to leave behind school theories and start learning life lessons.

I think about that a lot in these days of so-called online communities. Today's citizen journalism means that anyone can blog his or her own news. Yet, I'm struck that instead of thinking more about people's feelings, writers today seem to care even less than we did in the old days. So much meanness and pettiness permeates today's Web site postings; it'll be interesting to see if that changes as the Web matures.

So with the senator's return what had been a winter of exciting change turned into a spring and summer of retrenchment and learning how to manage a diverse staff and work with a variety of personality types. My new hires left one by one. One night, one of them, despondent over a breakup with his girlfriend, got in his car after a village board meeting and just started driving. He ended up in California a few days later. None of us knew what had happened to him for weeks, until he wrote asking for his last paycheck (he eventually made his career as a public relations person). We reconnected a few years ago in a business setting, which was when I finally heard the full story of why he had disappeared on me so many years before.

A woman I'd hired didn't show up at work one day (a strange but increasingly common occurrence there). I got hold of her two days later to have her tell me she'd been diagnosed with skin cancer and had been too upset to come to work or call to tell me. She survived the cancer but found another job that took her away from our little VW newsroom. My third hire, who'd been our sports editor, also left shortly after he and I were among the first at the scene of a massive DC-10 jet crash at O'Hare airport that year.

I can remember that May day as if it just happened. The sports editor, Norm, and I were having a late Friday lunch at a local Chinese place. Friday was normally a slow day in our cycle since the papers we published were delivered on Thursdays. As we came out of the restaurant, we saw a giant plume of smoke coming for the direction of the local high school. I asked Norm if he had cameras in his car (he doubled as a staff photographer). He said he did. We swung by the office to tell them we were going toward the smoke and to get people there onto finding out what was happening. Norm just kept driving, all the way to O'Hare, not far from our offices. Norm followed a fire engine past police barricades with us screaming press to the stunned cops trying to stop us, until we arrived at the horrific scene.

Only moments after American Airlines Flight 191 had taken off, an engine fell off its left wing. The jet flipped sideways and plowed into an empty field across the road from the runway, killing all 271 people on board and two people on the ground. When

Norm and I arrived, emergency workers were walking through a field whose grass had been scorched black. There were no huge airplane parts to be seen anywhere; it literally had disintegrated from the force of the crash.

The only thing I could recognize looking around was a piece of the plane's tail. A giant trench had been created by the plane's wing, I supposed, and the trench too was charred and singed brown. The workers were sticking small yellow flags into the ground in seemingly random patterns. I asked one what he was doing. Marking remains of the dead, he told me. Looking at where he had put flags, my untrained eye couldn't see anything that looked like a body, let alone body parts.

We did what journalists do at tragedies; we went to work taking photos of everything and anything. I also wandered around looking for a phone booth (this was before cell phones, as were so many of my journalism adventures), found one and called the office to tell them. They by now had heard details on the radio and were wondering what to do. I instructed them to get a passengers' list and look for locals. That's what small papers do in the face of a major disaster. We report on the local angle.

Norm and I returned to the newsroom and got to work developing the film (this was pre-digital camera) and printing photos of the crash site well into the night. I had trouble sleeping for weeks; I saw those images again and again every time I shut my eyes. That crash taught me at a very young age some of life's fragility and made me more aware of the pettiness of some of the things that upset us. None of those passengers expected to die that day. I didn't know who they were, but I think of them every time I'm at O'Hare. And I think of them every time I take a flight, such as on a recent one that sent me to London. Every day is a gift, I'm reminded. The gifts stopped for them that day in 1979.

It was a long summer. I wrote many stories about the aftermath of that crash and dealing daily with the back and forth between Junior and the senator. Then, one day in the early fall, I came in to work only to have Junior pull me aside. "Come outside with me for a minute," he said. He then walked me to the parking lot and pointed to a new Mercedes two-seater convertible. He'd bought a new car. Great but why was he starting my day with this, I wondered. He quickly told me. He'd bought the new car with part of his portion of the proceeds – the senator had sold the company to a larger chain of suburban newspapers!

Seems the senator just couldn't trust Junior to run the paper and so decided to sell while the market was good. This was my second time working for a family-run company but the first time I'd experienced working in the midst of the family's conflict about how to run their company. Years later, I would work for a magazine publishing company run by three brothers who, we were told, never spoke to each other. Each oversaw one area of the company but couldn't stand working with the others. They too were second generation owners, so it might be wise to avoid companies being run by the offspring of the founders.

The senator had arranged for the buyers to agree to keep Junior on as general manager. The rest of us would just have to wait and see what the new owners had planned for us.

Soon we went through orientation at our new owner's headquarters and were told not to worry. But I heard from friends who worked for the new owner that my job was already being advertised in their newsroom. New owners like to put their own people in charge of companies they buy. I've lived through this and written about it in countless corporate takeover stories. I wasn't as sure about this truism then as I am now, but my advice to anyone in a senior role during a takeover: start job hunting.

I put together a new resume and started looking. I wasn't quite prepared for how I would actually lose my job, though. It seems Junior felt the pressure of having real bosses instead of working for his dad. One week, as the paper's sales team worked to create an ad supplement for a big advertiser, he came in and told me my staff would need to work Saturday to proofread the supplement so that it could be published on time. I said this was ridiculous.

My reporters already worked many late nights covering various meetings in addition to all their other reporting; proofreading ad copy wasn't work for editors, and certainly not on their day off. If he wanted them to work on Saturday, he'd have to pay them as freelance proofreaders. We started arguing in the middle of our tiny newsroom, with everyone listening of course. He told me about all the pressures he was under from the new owners but all I could think about was that Mercedes. Finally, he said he was the boss and I had to listen to him.

"Or what? You'll fire me? You don't have the balls to fire me!" I screamed (I know, stupid, but I was only 26 at the time). He fired me on the spot. I grabbed what belongings I could from my desk, including the story list for that week's editions that were essential for physically putting the papers together, and stormed out of the office, never to return.

I found out later that the senator hit the ceiling when he heard, mad that since Junior had fired me, the company now had to pay me unemployment insurance.

I was 26, out of work, and not very likely to get a favorable recommendation from my most recent employer. Now what?

I'd already been testing the job waters since the company's sale but now I went into full job search mode. I reverted to techniques from my college days, daily scanning newspapers ads, answering ads across the country. My resume stated that I'd lost my most recent job after the company had been taken over and I left it at that. Given all the corporate takeovers that occur these days, I think that's still the way I would advise anyone caught in a similar situation to phrase their situation. I would have been fired sooner or later anyway, my actions just sped up the process.

I also applied for journalism teaching positions and indeed, received an offer to teach at Kent State University in Ohio. Although I was out of work, I decided to turn that position down, though. I just didn't feel that I had enough work experience to teach journalism. I was only three years out of grad school. What could I really teach except maybe how to lose a job by insulting your boss?

Each day I sent two to five letters to potential employers but time seemed to drag. After about a month, as I sat at home one day watching TV I began watching "It's a Wonderful Life," a movie that I'd never seen before but which has since become a Christmas classic. I loved the story about the feisty little local savings & loan going up against the town's evil banker. The movie brightened what was a very dark time for me.

Then, a few days later, I received a call from a blind ad – one where the employer isn't mentioned – that I'd answered. The U.S. League of Savings & Loans, the trade group for S&Ls, then based in Chicago, needed an assistant editor for its magazine. Here was life imitating art, as far as I was concerned. Seeing "It's a Wonderful Life" when I did was a sign that this was the job for me.

I went to the interview and played up all the reporting on the housing and mortgage markets I'd done in both my jobs. The housing market was booming then and was the biggest business news story in the suburbs. I mentioned my summers on Wall Street and how I enjoyed writing about markets in general. That all fit with what they were looking for. Not only did the magazine, *Savings & Loan News*, write about housing and mortgages, but it also was soon to be writing about new investing powers S&Ls were asking for. Some of those included trading mortgage-backed securities, a type then called Ginnie Maes, named after the government agency that created the securities. The job offer came just before Christmas – timed like the movie! – and after six weeks of unemployment, I was again working as a journalist.

This switch to magazines from newspapers meant I'd write long-form feature stories. The reporting and writing for the Saturday magazine that

I'd done at my first job on my own time came in handy. Indeed, samples of that writing helped me get the new job. But I recognized that the big challenge would be changing how I thought of myself as a journalist. The new job would take me back to business writing. What about my political reporting ambitions? To have a job, I was willing to take on the new challenge and leave behind the old days and dreams.

Lessons for You:

✓ Know the hidden costs of working for a family business.

✓ Don't trash talk your boss; he'll fire you. Try to have a plan before you leave.

✓ Be ready and willing to give up old dreams for exciting new challenges. Or a paycheck.

Chapter 5

Switching Specialties

Switching specialties within a career can be difficult. I was too naïve when I switched to magazine from newspaper reporting and writing. I didn't think there'd be much of a difference. After all, I'd written longer newspaper feature stories, how different could magazine writing be?

Very different, as I soon found out. I rushed through my first few assignments thinking I was doing fine. Until the day I ran into the publisher, in the men's room, a wonderful man who would soon retire, who asked me how things were going. I said fine, but offered that I felt like I didn't have enough work. He gently suggested it would be ok to take a little more time with my stories. Eventually, I came to realize what he meant. Magazine writing and reporting is a world away from newspaper work. I had to learn a new specialty within my chosen profession.

While I might interview three or four people for a local newspaper story I now worked for a national publication and, to get a national perspective, I might interview 15, 20 or more people for a feature story. This many interviews meant organizing mountains of notes. In my first newspaper job I often organized and wrote 500 word stories in my head as I called in from village board meetings. Now I was writing 2,000 to 3,000-word stories.

It was a challenge. I needed a narrative theme for a feature story, along with supporting data, and a flair for story telling that often wasn't needed in a typical newspaper story that contained "just the facts."

How did I tackle this? I read as many back issues of my new magazine as I could get my hands on and deconstructed other people's stories to see what approaches they had taken. I went back to my notes from a grad school magazine writing class to find tips on how to organize my notes – tips I use to this very day. For the first time, I rewrote my work; there normally isn't time to rewrite a newspaper story. I also took time to discuss my work with my editors and my peers. I was lucky; this was the heyday of trade magazines and we counted an editor, two senior editors, two associate editors and two assistant editors on staff. Today, a magazine is lucky to have two staffers, so it's much harder to learn from your peers, much less your editor.

I also volunteered to cover new beats. I taught myself enough about technology to write pieces on IT and the computer systems that S&Ls used. When S&Ls got regulatory authority to start trading financial futures contracts, I volunteered to cover this as well. My fascination with Wall Street hadn't faded. Covering financial futures markets, then centered in Chicago, seemed like fun.

As it turned out, learning to cover financial futures led to my next job, the only job I've ever been recruited for. I was happy at *S&L News*, so happy I began to wonder if I would actually want to spend the rest of my career there instead of moving up to the next level of my profession. I'd already turned down one job at a new weekly business publication in Chicago and wondered if that had been a mistake.

Most people likely wouldn't worry about being happy in a job. Isn't that what we all want, after all? So let me explain why I was worried in that job. It was still early in my professional life and I wanted to continue to advance in my profession, to the top level of journalism. I did not want to become complacent working for a trade magazine, no matter how good it was or how wonderful my coworkers and the working environment was.

Later in my career, I would be at positions where I started job hunting because I could sense troubles were on the horizon for the company I was at. Troubles would eventually come to this workplace as well, but I did not see that at the time. Quite the opposite, I was concerned I could get comfortable staying there for 20 or 30 years and so never experience the parts of my profession that would take me to the big-time.

At around this time, late 1982 or early 1983 as I recall, I met the Chicago bureau chief of Reuters, the British newswire service, at a press luncheon at the Chicago Board of Trade. Reuters, now known as Thomson Reuters, was much smaller in the United States then. In fact, it was just beginning to expand its U.S. presence, primarily by covering business news. Its Chicago bureau covered commodity futures trading in commodities such as wheat, soybeans and pork bellies. But the growing financial futures markets meant Reuters needed to expand its staff to cover those as well. Trouble was, few reporters knew anything about financial futures. So when the bureau chief heard I'd been covering the futures markets, he immediately invited me to his office to discuss a job. That still has to be one of the coolest days of my professional life.

Suddenly I was in demand. Better yet, Reuters reporters were unionized. No need to negotiate a salary; we just looked at the contract terms to see where I fit in the pay scale – and it was a very nice fit. Reuters would pay me 30 percent more than the S&L trade magazine. As in most professions, this is what happens when you move up a level, in my case from a national trade or association magazine to an international news service. It was too good an offer to turn down.

I felt badly about leaving the friends I had made at *S&L News* and wondered if I was making a mistake. It was 1983 and *S&L News* and the association that published it seemed like it would be around for the next hundred years. And there I was, again, moving to change specialties, to go from the magazine writer I was becoming to be a wire service reporter, someone who would file six to eight reports a day on financial futures markets, new markets that few people understood.

Was I crazy? I hope not, an opportunity had come along that I didn't expect to get for years. I had to jump at the chance, to see if I could make it in the big show. Don't fear such chances, the older you become, the more you'll realize how rare they truly are.

A decade later, the association and its *S&L News* no longer existed, victims of the S&L financial collapse of the 1980s. Several of my former colleagues, friends who'd stayed put, found themselves out of work, stunned by the end of an employer – and an industry – that had seemed rock solid.

The end of that association was the first time I personally experienced just how unsure the business world is. You can never, never think your employer will be around forever, or at least as long as you hope to work there. Businesses come and go everyday, you have to protect yourself, do not depend on a business to do it.

Lessons for You:

✓ Changing specialties is challenging but can help you later in your career.

✓ When the Big Time comes calling, answer the knock at your door.

✓ No employer lasts forever, always consider your career goals first.

Chapter 6

Making it to the Big Time

Moving to Reuters from a trade magazine was like moving up to the big leagues from the minor leagues. Like most professions, journalism has several levels. In giant corporations, a similar move occurs when someone in charge of a formerly back-water division suddenly has to manage dramatic growth – and expectations – and gets transferred to corporate headquarters.

Back then, circa 1983, the classic journalism career path meant starting at a small newspaper working your way up to a big city daily, like the *New York Times*. I imagined the same for myself although writing for the *New York Daily News* was my dream. My working-class family read the *News*, not the more up-scale *Times*. When I had to buy and read the *Sunday Times* for my high school political science class, my family was more shocked than anything else.

But back to my career path. As I've written already, the path of moving up the newspaper chain was one I had left when I switched to the world of trade magazines. Even within that world, there's a hierarchy. Association magazines are normally looked down upon by other trader journalists because, most times, they're used merely as public relations and lobbying tools and don't involve much real journalism. I'd been fortunate to work for an association that allowed its editors and writers to be real journalists. Topics of stories there were decided upon by the editors and few topics were taboo. The public relations aspects of what we wrote were not discussed. We were doing service journalism, trying to help our readers be better at their jobs, an approach I also would take toward trade magazine journalism later in my career.

But that said, going to Reuters was an entirely different world. First, my salary cracked the $30,000 a year mark, which had seemed only a distant possibility when I was at a trade magazine. (this was in 1983, by the way, when $30,000 went farther than it does today). Reuters at the time was unionized, a result of its first U.S. bureau being in New York City. I joined the New York Newspaper Guild because it was the union that first unionized Reuters. Unions are now demonized and blamed for everything from the fall of the U.S. economy to the government's ineffectiveness. My reaction? I've never had as good a salary or as many benefits as I did when I was in the Guild. N one person has the bargaining power that all employees speaking as one have.

Reuters also paid me overtime, thanks to my union contract. No publication before or since has done that. It paid me double time when I worked weekends, something I did extensively in 1984 when Continental Illinois Bank, then the second largest bank in Illinois, failed and I was assigned to write about it every day for a month straight. I was already learning that without a union, an individual has zero negotiating leverage against a company.

My Reuters days were heady ones. I'm on the right here, sitting with my editor at the time and his date. My then editor, now friend, Tony and I today do our own blog, guysandgoodhealth.com.

My experience has been that companies will let you quit rather than agree to increase your salary. I've seen this happen many times. The only time you're in any sort of bargaining position is when you're being hired. If a company really wants you, it may meet a demand you make for a pay higher than its initial offer. Although even that is not certain.

In 2005, I had been extended a job offer at a Chicago company that publishes magazines for trade groups and companies. The offer was $10,000 less than my previous salary. I asked for $10,000 more and the company withdrew its offer. A few years later I ended up applying to this same company for a different position but after a first interview I changed my mind. I couldn't work for a company that didn't fully value my work.

But Reuters' higher salary and those benefits came with tremendous pressure to be a first-rate journalist for its international readers. Instead of having weeks to research long features, I needed to quickly learn everything I could about financial futures contracts – what they are, who buys and sells them, and what factors impact prices and market movement. This didn't mean reading books. I had to learn everything from my sources as they were working on Chicago's loud, chaotic trading floors. I had to persuade them to talk to me every day, to tell me what was happening in the markets and why. I then wrote, or in Reuters vernacular, filed, five stories throughout the day on the markets I covered. Many times, market activity was so hectic that I didn't have time to get back to my desk and write my stories; I'd call up from the trading floor and dictate a story without any time to write it out first; many times I lost my voice by the end of the day from literally screaming into the phone so I could be heard over the tremendous din of the trading floor.

And unlike other reporters, I wasn't covering one or two markets, I covered all financial futures. The markets were so new in 1983 that I was the first and for a time, the only Reuters reporter covering this beat in Chicago. I rapidly learned about U.S. Treasury bonds, bills and notes, Eurodollars (basically U.S. dollars held overseas upon which people traded futures contracts to buy or sell them) and foreign currencies like the Deutsche Mark, French Franc and Japanese Yen (this was long before the Euro). The contracts were traded at two different exchanges, the Chicago Board of Trade and the Chicago Mercantile Exchange, located about four blocks apart on the western fringes of Chicago's Loop business district, which meant I had to continuously run between the two buildings. The two have recently merged and the new, consolidated trading is largely electronic today, so the world I covered in the 1980s is largely gone, and likely forgotten by all but those who were down there every day, some making millions, some losing millions, and some, like me, making $30,000 to report on it all.

When I covered them, financial futures contracts were traded in massive, crowded pits at each exchange. I ran between them all day, quickly dropping my coat off in offices we had in each building and then heading to the trading floors to get people down there to tell me what was going on.

Who read my stories? Bankers, insurance company traders, investment bankers, anyone who used these sophisticated financial instruments to protect their investments from unexpected market risks like interest rate spikes, a housing market collapse or a foreign crisis. Throughout the day, my stories appeared in offices around the world on what today seems like very primitive printers. Reuters used its own word processing system because personal computers were not yet ubiquitous in American business. Businesses were just beginning to switch to desktop computers – the sight of investment pros staring at a wall of screens full of numbers and commentary was just around the corner. Indeed, the day of the news service printer already had passed eight years later in 1991 and 1992, when I became Chicago bureau chief of a competing news service, Knight Ridder Financial News (no longer in business).

Suffice it to say, my days were very busy. I started work at 7:30 and was usually finished by 4 but between these hours I rarely sat still and was constantly talking to someone, writing five to seven daily market reports or my longer twice-weekly analysis pieces or features on traders who already were, or were about to become, famous.

The trading floors, with as many as 500 people squeezed into a hexagonal trading pit screaming, pushing and begging to make money off of each other, reminded me of a New York street fight, so in an odd way I felt at home. These traders, overwhelming men, usually came from Chicago's neighborhoods straight to the exchanges. Many hadn't gone to college but instead had started their careers as clerks and messengers on the trading floor, working their way into trading jobs that could make them wealthy beyond their dreams, or send them crashing into bankruptcy with one bad trade. The exchanges hated it when reporters called these guys gamblers, preferring to talk about the economic risk management function that trading offered the markets. But really, most of them were wild-men gamblers. Their weekend trips to Las Vegas, often on privately chartered jets, were testament to that. The way traders threw money at women, drugs, parties, houses, boats, and even expeditions to find the remains of Marco Polo (one trader was a history buff) was legendary. And there I was, a $30,000-a-year reporter, getting pushed, kicked, yelled at and spat on, as I tried to learn the markets and write stories that helped other people get wealthy or at least stay that way. Yes, I earned that raise Reuters gave me.

I was constantly afraid while I covered the markets. Not of the people or the chaos, but that I'd miss a huge, market-moving story. Afraid that I didn't have enough good sources on the floors to know what was really going on, afraid I couldn't develop more sources, afraid sources were lying to me to benefit their own trading positions. Was I paranoid? Not at all.

Years later, when I was at Knight-Ridder, one of my reporters misquoted the then U.S. treasury secretary regarding the strength of the dollar. She reported the exact opposite of what he said during his mid-day appearance in Chicago. Markets reacted immediately. It took us eight minutes to realize and correct the mistake. In that time, Knight-Ridder subscribers lost hundreds of thousands, if not millions, of dollars trading on bad information. The company itself likely lost tens of thousands of dollars in canceled subscriptions. That's what it's like in the big time.

Just when I thought I couldn't be any more afraid of making a mistake, something even bigger hit my world. Continental Illinois, which I mentioned earlier, began to fail as its bad loans to Oklahoma and Texas oil industry companies and individuals turned south. Bank failures are now so commonplace that we may have become immune to such news, but back in 1984 the idea that a major U.S. bank had gone crazy making bad loans was big, big news.

The scandal had started with the failure of a small Oklahoma bank but soon the news surfaced that Continental had bought loans made through that bank, and the dominoes began to topple, straight toward Continental's headquarters at the foot of LaSalle Street. I first heard about the bank's impending failure on the trading floors when the interest rates investors demanded for buying Continental's certificates of deposits and other financial instruments started going up. Investors were losing faith in Continental's ability to stay in business. As the story grew, my bureau chief told me that I was covering it full-time. My background writing about savings and loans meant I knew more about the banking system and its regulations than anyone else in the bureau. A reporter who worked part-time at the bureau would work on the story with me. The two of us had to keep digging and keep finding out what was really going on.

Our competitors like *The Wall Street Journal* and its Dow Jones news service seemed to have scores of reporters on the same story. I literally worked day and night, and weekends. I remember on Sunday pounding out stories in a stuffy office when the building and its air conditioners were shut down. My bureau chief edited over my shoulder so the story could be ready before the markets opened in Tokyo the next morning there. It was about a month before the bank actually failed and the U.S. government took it over.

This was likely the biggest story of my journalism career. I'd both scooped my competitors during that month and I'd been beaten on stories at times. Overall, Reuters coverage was solid; we were on the story, on an almost minute by minute basis at times.

Coverage continued. When a shareholders' meeting was held in an auditorium at the Art Institute of Chicago to approve a reorganization plan for the bank, my then three-person team of Reuters reporters beat Dow Jones and the *Journal* with the story by disabling all but one of the pay phones located outside the meeting room. We didn't let other reporters use that one working phone. One of us would keep the line open to the Reuters bureau while the other two ran in and out of the meeting, taking notes and then calling in more news. We beat the first Dow Jones news report on that meeting by eight minutes that day. In breaking news – like in today's 24/7 online news sites – where scoops are counted in seconds, eight minutes was (and still is) a huge margin. When we returned to the bureau, our colleagues greeted us with a standing ovation because of those eight minutes.

Despite being frightened all the time, I loved those moments. I got one more big scoop that day, when I reported on the bank's layoff plans. I'd looked over the shoulder of a Continental executive, who for some reason was casually paging through a reorganization plan at the meeting while sitting surrounded by reporters, and I saw, and madly copied down the numbers of planned layoffs. I was the only one who noticed, and later called the bank for confirmation, before writing my story.

After covering Continental's implosion, covering the markets seemed almost dull by comparison. What's worse, after my month away, some of my sources were no longer on the trading floors and I was completely out of sync with the market's rhythms.

My Reuters job also was starting to affect my marriage. I'd married another journalist; we'd met in college. Almost from the start, the fact that we were both trying to make it in the same profession strained our marriage. When I made the leap to the big time with Reuters, my wife, who felt stalled in her career, began re-examining what she really wanted to do with her life. The more attention I received professionally, the worse the strain became. Then she decided that it was time for us to have children, something she had adamantly said that she didn't want to do when we had married in 1977.

I wanted to wait a while to start a family. I was enjoying the spotlight, and the partying and drinking bouts that went with it. But by early 1984, I'd agreed to the baby request and also agreed to find a less stressful job that would allow me to be home more. It would be the first, but not the last time, I would put family ahead of career. Balancing family and career is a constant struggle for anyone working today. My hat's off to people who do it without hurting their careers or their marriages. In my case, career compromises I made would haunt me the rest of my working life. And the marriage ended anyway, in 1993, pulled down by many things, including career.

But, in 1984, in an incredibly fortuitous development, I discovered that *BusinessWeek*, then one of the country's major business magazines, needed someone to cover the Chicago financial markets since its market reporter was transferring overseas. Networking was key here, a lesson for job hunters today. I had become friends with a public relations woman at the Chicago Mercantile Exchange who knew everyone covering the markets. She mentioned that the *BusinessWeek* reporter, who I did not know except by her byline, was leaving soon. That was all I needed to hear, I was applying to *BusinessWeek* the same evening.

In those days, *BusinessWeek's* Chicago bureau, staffed with five people, was one of its largest. Usually writers started working for *BusinessWeek* at smaller bureaus in places like Atlanta or Boston and only then worked their way to Chicago and, eventually, to headquarters in New York. The magazine almost never hired local Chicago business writers. But luckily, the new Chicago bureau chief wanted someone who knew the markets. He believed it would be easier to train someone how to write in *BusinessWeek* style than it would be to train one of the magazine's writers to cover the markets, which he himself knew enough about from a previous stint in Chicago to know that he wanted a specialist to cover them.

So he pushed for hiring me. I found out years later that he actually rewrote my writing test so it sounded enough like *BusinessWeek* style to convince his New York bosses to hire me. Thank you Jim, I don't think I've ever publicly thanked you for that.

I started work one month before my son was born in December 1984. I was still in the big leagues and those were incredibly heady times. My first day on the job, I flew to New York to attend a massive party that night at the Plaza Hotel given for *BusinessWeek's* then new editor-in-chief. Reuters was the big time, but reporting and writing stories there was trench warfare. Working at *BusinessWeek* was like being a member of an elite club, more akin to being an Air Force pilot than a foot soldier. I took my parents to lunch that day in New York, thinking they'd be amazingly proud of me making it to *BusinessWeek* after only eight years as a journalist. Instead, my dad took me aside and told me how worried they both were that I kept changing jobs! When would I settle down in one job, he asked. If only he knew.

BusinessWeek in the 1980s was undoubtedly the best place I ever worked. Leaving there was likely the biggest mistake I ever made but I did it to try to save my then young family. It didn't work. The irony is that many people who stayed from my era lost their jobs in 2009 when Bloomberg bought *BusinessWeek*. So if I had stayed, I would have been unemployed during this horrific recession anyway.

But back to 1984. In less than two years after I had joined the *BusinessWeek* staff, my dad had died of a heart attack and I'd left the big time in what, ultimately, was a failed attempt to save my marriage. I've spent the rest of my career back in the minor leagues, trying to fit in as a big fish in small ponds but more often than not realizing that there just wasn't enough oxygen in those ponds for me to keep breathing professionally.

Can you prevent a high-pressure job from hurting your personal life? Can you have both a successful career and a successful family life? Usually this is a question women wrestle with but I think men think about it too, even if we don't talk about it as much.

Are there jobs you should leave if they adversely impact your family? Or particularly in today's tough job market, should family members understand that in order to reach the top of your profession it means they have to give you some leeway?

This was such a conflicted time for me; the happiest time of my professional life and yet, the beginning of 10 years of personal tragedies and conflict that ended in my divorce. We all, including our children, still deal with the pain we went through. But

I think this chapter raises some of the serious issues many people face in trying to balance career and family, all issues that are part of the job-hunting mix.

Lessons for You:

✓ Negotiate your salary. You may be overjoyed to get a job and want to quickly settle the money matters and start work. But remember, this may be not just the best but the only time you can ask for what you deserve.

✓ Don't lose sight of the big picture. Is your job security worth the price of your marriage and stable family life? It may be, temporarily. But try to understand the long-term costs and benefits. This is particularly true in commuting long distances to keep a job or land a new one.

✓ If you make it to the top levels of your profession, don't walk away unless you're sure you'll never regret that decision. Getting back to the top is almost impossible once you leave.

Chapter 7

The Early-Career Crisis

My years at *BusinessWeek* were truly the best and worst of times. My father died in early 1986, a little more than a year after I started at *BW*. That, in turn, led to the beginning of the end of my marriage, partly because my father died of a heart attack after one of countless fights he had with my-then wife, who could never stomach my parents and what she called their "blue collar gauche" ways.

Friends advised me to divorce her then but the good Catholic boy in me was determined to somehow hang on to the marriage. My first test of that approach came in 1987 when *BusinessWeek* wanted to transfer me to another bureau. That was the routine; spend three years in one city then move on. My application included the fact that I'd minored in German so going to *BusinessWeek*'s Germany bureau was a possible option. I could have been there when the Wall tumbled and Germany was reunited, an amazing story for anyone who grew up in the Cold War years, as I did. But my spouse reacted to a transfer with an ultimatum – if I went to another city for *BusinessWeek*, I went alone. She would not leave a new business she and a partner were starting up in Chicago (a business which six years later when we were going through divorce was valued as worthless, by the way). Trying to save my marriage, I looked for another way to find a job in Chicago.

BusinessWeek never outright said that if I didn't transfer (after I'd said no to Germany, the magazine offered a Toronto posting and I turned it down, too) that I'd eventually be fired but I felt it was looming over me and so I quit *BusinessWeek*. A reporter friend and I decided to start our own newsletter publishing company, convinced people would pay us large sums of money to read our commentaries on the futures markets. We planned to write about how banks and savings & loans could use futures to hedge interest rate risks.

Unfortunately, we started up just before a major stock market collapse in late 1987. We soon spent more time trying to raise capital to keep the company going than reporting or writing. We also tried selling bulk newsletter subscriptions to brokerage firms for their clients but I found out that selling is definitely not a skill I possess. By late 1988, it was clear we weren't going to survive, so we sold off our subscribers and returned about 10 cents on the dollar to our investors (ourselves included) and felt fortunate we didn't have any major outstanding company debts to pay off.

I learned some important lessons during that time. Namely, that I love working for myself. But I also learned I couldn't run a company alone. I needed a sales partner to convince people of the value of my writing. (I've been thinking about that a lot as I begin selling this book. Hopefully I'm better at selling now than I once was.)

By mid-1988, I knew I needed to find another job and quickly found that employers worry about hiring someone who has worked on their own. Attitudes may be different now, but in those days independent thinkers were hardly on the top of most hiring lists. At the time, one of the main characters on a popular television show, "thirtysomething" went through a similar situation. His ad agency had failed and he was going hat in hand to larger agencies begging for a job, only to be rebuffed again and again. His marriage also was breaking up, leading me to wonder if the show's writers had hidden cameras in my house to get some of their script ideas.

I knew *BusinessWeek* wouldn't take me back and I wasn't anxious to go back to the daily reporting grind of Reuters. I also realized that after working on my own, I wasn't pining for another boss. Besides, I wasn't even sure I wanted to still be a journalist. I was 35 years old and 11 years out of grad school, which seemed then like a very long time.

I felt a mid-life crisis approaching, although of course, I was well short of mid-career. I always tend to project ahead a bit.

Now I began to wonder what else I might like to do. To write and create my newsletter I'd bought an early PC and used the first version of a layout program called PageMaker (now in version 7.0). The revolution in publications creation had just begun. Then, it affected the mechanical and physical way publications were put together as companies moved from lines of lead type to words on computer screens that eventually became printed pages. Today, the revolution continues as businesses fight to sign up subscribers and find new ways to make money since, today, print advertising is disappearing.

My PageMaker experience made me an early expert – I even taught a class at a Chicago-area university – in what was then called desktop publishing. Thinking I could find a job related to desktop publishing, I approached both the Chicago Mercantile Exchange and the Chicago Board of Trade. I knew they each sent out a number of newsletters and other publications and marketing materials and I told them they could save by leaving traditional typesetting and printing. I also pitched my writing skills, thinking I'd try writing executive speeches and leave my reporting days.

The Merc hired me for its public affairs department, so I didn't feel as thought I'd sold out my journalism career to become a PR man. But my job ended up being even more excoriating than I imagined straight PR could've been.

Public affairs dealt with exchange members and political stakeholders. I oversaw the Merc's political action committee newsletter, for example, a lobbying tool aimed directly at Washington decision makers. I also wrote speeches for the chairman and the president of the exchange. Speech writing wasn't satisfying at all. As a reporter, I was accustomed to seeing my byline on everything I wrote. If I wrote insights, people thought I was insightful, and I liked that. A lot. Overall, journalism doesn't pay much. But its practitioners like to see their names attached to their work and they like people thinking that they're smart. I once heard ad man Donny Deutsch tell a group of reporters that he always tried to be nice to them because he knew that they resented him. After all, they'd all made better grades than him but he made money in advertising while they were poorly paid. Thanks Donny.

No one was nice to writers at the Merc. We weren't there for people to know how smart we were, we were there to make our bosses and their bosses look smart. So when I wrote a speech for the chairman, which he got kudos for, I wasn't supposed to tell people I wrote the speech and that he'd only looked at it 10 minutes before delivering it. My job was to make people think he was brilliant. Now, in all fairness, he was an extremely bright fellow and he did some amazing things in elevating the Merc to be a world financial player from a sleepy little club, but that really didn't make it any easier for me.

My boss at the Merc was the sister of a former Chicago mayor. A political person, she was accustomed to political staffers being seen and not heard, which also rankled me tremendously since I'd been accustomed to almost constant positive feedback every time I wrote a good story. After only a few weeks, I realized I'd made a terrible job decision. A talk with the head of human resources helped me realize that I was now working in an environment where staff recognition really was not part of the workplace DNA. Staff existed to contribute to the senior executives' reputations and to that of the exchange itself; we were all supposed to derive our job satisfaction from what the world thought about the Merc.

To be fair, the Merc is far from the only place that operates with this model; in fact, most large corporations do, too. I'd written about it but never experienced it and adjusting to this culture change was the most difficult part of trying to switch fields.

I tried to ignore it by building up the other part of my job, the desktop publishing side. I created a user group of people from the various exchange departments who produced newsletters and held regular meetings aimed at standardizing newsletter styles, formats and typefaces to produce a consistent Merc look. We even brought in representatives from NeXT, Steve Jobs' company, to demo their new machines for us. I was doing what I had to do – writing speeches, annual reports and newsletters – but enjoying being the leader of my user group. Until the day my boss called me and ordered me to disband the group. What I saw as helping the Merc create a consistent style for its publications, she saw as empire building, exactly the words she used in reading me the riot act to stop. That's when I knew I had to get out of there.

I worked at the Merc for exactly one year and 10 days. I was so disheartened. I counted every day and more than 20 years later remember the count. That job convinced me I was a journalist, not just a writer who was content to put words in other people's mouths. A few years later I would again work in the Merc's building as Chicago bureau chief for Knight-Ridder Financial News. The contrast between the two jobs couldn't have been starker or a better reminder that finding a job that fits who I am is the most important thing.

I'd give you the same advice. Do you want to be a star at work? Then find a company that recognizes stars and encourages people to stand out. Are you more comfortable at part of a team effort? Then look for a team environment – and be sure to ask about teamwork when you're interviewing. Are you content to be in the background while others get the glory? Then find that type of workplace. Know which works for you. Being the wrong person in the wrong type of business environment is deadly for your morale, your productivity and, ultimately I think, for your health as well.

Lessons for You:

✓ Running your own company requires skills you may not have.

✓ Know what rewards you need from a job, either money, fame, recognition, and be sure a new job offers that.

✓ Switching jobs isn't always the answer for family problems.

Chapter 8

Joining the Work-at-Home Movement

The early 1990s, for me, were simultaneously a time of job-hopping gone wild and the slow death of my marriage. The two were related, I'm sure. The less happy I felt at home, the more I looked to work to supply enjoyment and people I wanted to be around and to talk with each day. When you start your day trying to find a reason to get up each morning and then you dread going home each night from your office, your work can take on way too large a role in your life. No job can truly compensate for a miserable home life.

I left the Merc for a trade magazine that covered the meat, poultry and seafood businesses. As it turned out, my first magazine editor from my savings and loan days was consulting for the publication. He had been tasked with finding a new editor for the magazine and so he'd run an ad in the *Chicago Tribune* (newspaper want ads seem quaint now, don't they?) to find a new editor and I answered the ad during one of those 375 days I spent at the Merc. While executive search experts these days say you can't find a new job from ads, I have found several that way, even recently. The ads are online now, on career-specific sites. I still advise checking ads frequently when you're job hunting.

During a recession in 1991, the company publishing my meat magazine couldn't sell its real estate holdings to refinance its magazine business. So the meat magazine was put up for sale.

I was truly sad to leave that job because I had been able to assemble a staff with people I truly came to care about as wonderful friends. One would subsequently help me find a job several years later. The other has reappeared in my life more recently thanks to social networking and has given me a LinkedIn recommendation that has helped me in more recent job searches. I, in turn, gave her a recommendation that helped her secure a new spot after she decided to leave her real estate career behind. Working with people you like and respect is one of the true gifts of any career. If you find a place with people you love to see every day, think long and hard before leaving it.

I moved to Knight-Ridder to be its Chicago bureau chief in 1991, knowing that whoever bought the meat magazine would want an editor of his choosing (my replacement was fired by the new owners, by the way, not heeding my advice that he should find a new job before the magazine was sold). The Knight-Ridder bureau had 14 reporters but I was hired with the understanding that some of these reporters had simply been there too long and were no longer performing up to standards. My job was to improve them or document their short comings and fire them. When I worked for Reuters I'd known many of these people as friendly competitors, so basically, I took a job where I'd be encouraging friends to find other jobs. I justified that in my mind by wondering if some had simply become stale in what they were doing. I hoped I could motivate them to step up their games. Such are the choices, and the rationalizations, you make when looking for a job in a bad economy. My Knight-Ridder tenure was brutal as it coincided with the last years of my marriage. I couldn't find solace either at work or at home. But I was working for a stable, large company where I weathered the recession with a job, rather than without one.

By 1993, disgusted with being a hatchet man at Knight-Ridder and missing being able to work with a staff I could enjoy and befriend, I found a job with the company that had bought my old meat magazine where I now became the editor of its beverage magazine. It was an almost ideal position: I was able to choose and hire a new staff for the publication (the company had bought it from another publisher and moved it from Cleveland). I convinced a former coworker and friend to leave her job and become my managing editor, my No. 2 person. I also brought in one of my old friends from the meat magazine (whom I had hired there) to be our third editorial staffer. Leading a team who knew each other and shared the same journalism professional standards meant we started doing great work from the first issue we published.

Once again I had a job I looked forward to every day, and it balanced the sadness that surrounded my home life. My marriage ended that May and I signed a lease on a tiny efficiency apartment on what would've been our 16th wedding anniversary. The pain of an unhappy marriage was finally over but the pain of divorce, including worries about my two small children, was just beginning. I thought I was handling it all well, and work was such an island of calm, but I was wrong. By September, I couldn't take the sadness, pain and guilt over what I was doing to my children any longer and checked myself into the hospital to deal with extreme depression and suicidal thoughts. I had come to believe what my ex-wife had been telling me in heated arguments, namely that everyone would be better off without me in this world. It is difficult for me to believe how in the grips of depression I was then. I reached the depths of not wanting to live anymore, but somehow I knew I had to struggle back from that terrible precipice. I first checked into a hospital for help and subsequently spent months in intense therapy to regain myself and my self-respect.

My employers were incredibly supportive, as were my coworkers, who suddenly had to do my work as well as their own. I was only out of the office for one week while I was in the hospital but I'm sure my work wasn't up to par for quite a while after that. That time all seems so dark in my memory of it that it's difficult to write about it all, even now almost 20 years later. Are there lessons for job-hunters in all that? The biggest lesson is not to think that being depressed is normal, even if you find yourself surrounded by other depressed people. Lesson number two is that work is not a permanent escape from a depressed, troubled home life. Take care of yourself or you'll be no good to any employer, or yourself.

Unfortunately, this great job didn't last very much longer. By mid-1995, the company, which had started a new publication that wasn't doing well and so was dragging the company down with it, decided to sell one of its magazines. Since we covered beverages and the other magazines there covered food, we were put on the block. Knowing that new owners like to place their own people in key positions and rarely keep old editors, I started looking for work. Among my contacts, I found a friend of a friend who worked on a group of magazines that covered the growing business of bank credit and debit cards. The group was considering starting a new magazine in the new year, so I hoped it could turn into a job for me. I did not want to leave Chicago at that point, not wanting to abandon my children at such a difficult time, so my job search was limited to the Chicago area. Some friends and family encouraged me to move back to New York, where there were more journalism jobs to be had, and at larger, first-rate organizations, and where I had a family support system. It certainly would have been easier to get a fresh start. But I would have missed so much. I understand why so many divorced men will do that, move somewhere else, start anew and get away from their pain, but I have no regrets about staying in

Chicago and trying my best to stay involved in my children's lives.

My days at Beverage Industry were great because I had a great team. Here I am with team members Kristine and Dawn.

In early November my beverage magazine was sold. First the new owners told us, the staff, that they wanted to keep us all. But then they asked us to meet them one morning in an empty restaurant (except for us, the place was closed; it was like a scene right out of "The Godfather") where they offered to let us stay if we took 30 percent pay cuts.

I left that meeting and called the friend of a friend with whom I'd been discussing a new magazine. I told him that if he could beat my 30 percent pay cut offer, I'd launch his new magazine. He offered 10 percent below my then current pay and I accepted. As it turned out, at the last minute the sale of the beverage magazine feel through and the owner ended up selling the entire company to another publisher who actually kept him on. Then he somehow managed to sell the company for a third time. Those owners didn't want him to stay so he left and started a competing magazine publishing company, which he runs today.

The lesson? No job is secure. Companies that buy creative ventures never seem to understand that what they're actually buying isn't the final product like a magazine. They're actually buying the creativity of the employees. And that creativity, that human capital, can get up and walk out the door (and come back to haunt them) if they don't do everything possible to value it. But that's another book. For this book, the lesson is value your own talent and don't accept a garbage offer from a new owner. Start job hunting the second you know your company may be on the sales block.

I started with the banking group Jan. 3, 1996. For New Year's Day, I'd treated myself with a trip to Pasadena to watch my grad school alma mater play football. Northwestern University had accomplished the seeming impossible and had made it to the Rose Bowl as the Big Ten Conference champion that year, the first time since 1948. I'd booked the trip even before I knew I'd have the new job and so had to tell my new employers that I couldn't start until I returned from the Rose Bowl, which they found amusing from someone who'd almost been out of work. Seeing then perennial football doormat Northwestern rise to such heights inspired me to not get down in my job hunt at the time. The school, known primarily for academic excellence, has since gone on to have a fairly good football program, another reminder that any trend can be turned around.

My first year in that new job, with the help of freelance writers, I produced the new magazine on my own. The job was a bit more solitary than I liked, but during the second year I started building my own editorial team. All seemed well there until late 1998 when out of the blue, my editorial director told me that his boss, our division president, was firing one of our group so that he could meet quarterly earnings numbers. I was completely shocked. How could he make a decision like that without my input? What made the situation worse was that the staffer, an American who covered Asia, worked in Singapore. Firing him left him stranded there without a job or a way to get home. I wrote an angry e-mail to every senior person in the company blasting my division head for making the decision without consulting me or checking whether there might be another job for the dismissed staffer elsewhere in the company (it turned out there was).

That e-mail was a big mistake. It put me in the management doghouse after another senior executive told me it was the stupidest possible thing I could have done in that situation and that I wasn't likely to emerge from that doghouse. I started job hunting, again, and came across a very different kind of opportunity.

A British publisher was starting a U.S. trade magazine to cover the public relations profession. A co-worker of mine at the time knew the person in New York who'd been hired to recruit staffers for the new venture, including reporters across the country that could cover regional news while working from home offices. I'd worked from home doing my newsletter in the 1980s and so I knew I had the inner discipline it takes to use time productively despite distractions all around the house.

Focus is key in such a situation, as is having a defined work space and working out rules of behavior with your children beforehand so you can work and they know what that means in terms of not distracting you during your work hours.

My children were with me half the week at that point and quickly got into a routine of coming home from school and doing their homework while I finished my work day. When they were done, they would watch TV on the second floor of my town-house while I worked on the first.

My children and I went to see Northwestern play in the Citrus Bowl on New Year's Day 1997. Soon I would be working at home and they would be adjusting to that arrangement.

I'd given up my editor's title (indeed, I also gave up a second title as Associate Publisher, Editorial, since I oversaw newsletters and directories, as well), so I'd taken a step back professionally. I also had to take a 20 percent pay cut. Losing the title hurt a bit but I thought the benefits of being home would make this worth it. As for the income hit, I knew I could freelance while I worked from home since not commuting from my north suburban home into Chicago would net me two extra hours a day.

Working from home made my personal life easier to manage. I'd survived a grueling 18-month divorce battle to secure joint custody of my children and to be able to see them roughly half of each month. They lived with me every other Thursday through Sunday as well as visiting every week during the week. My son was in eighth grade and my daughter in fourth and I desperately wanted to stay involved in their lives. I coached my son in soccer and my daughter in basketball during their grade school years. Working from home made all this more doable, especially coaching my daughter's basketball games, which often started at 5 p.m. My kids could also come home after school rather than being in after-school care or home alone.

By 1998, I'd rebuilt my financial life with the help of loans from my mother and an aunt. I'd bought a three-bedroom duplex only eight blocks from my former marital home where the children lived half the time with their mother. It was important that their time with me didn't disrupt their school schedules or after-school activities, the reason I stayed so close.

During the days they lived with me, I drove them to school and sometimes picked them up and it took only a few minutes from my schedule. I began building a freelance business to make up for my lost income and started teaching journalism part-time at a local university on nights when I didn't have my children. It took juggling these three jobs to pay my bills, child support and a portion of the children's Catholic school tuition and healthcare costs that I had agreed to pay in order to secure joint custody. I was busy but honestly enjoyed having a lot to keep me occupied when the children weren't with me. As any divorced parent can tell you, the loneliness of those times can be overwhelming. I'd started dating as well, but that's *definitely* the topic of another book.

So if you've landed a new home-based job and you're telecommuting for the first time the big question is "What's it like to work at home?" It depends on the job and your personality. It can be isolating, although I was on the phone interviewing people for stories for a good part of every day so I did have human interaction. The writing part of being a journalist is by its nature a solitary act, so that I was used to. When I write I'm always alone even if I'm working in a crowded newsroom.

Keeping to a schedule wasn't difficult since I had specific deadlines for filing stories each week. I think any professional can keep focused on a job, even when home, if they are professional. What does this mean? For example, if you have children home, they need to understand that you have a defined place to work even if it's just the dining room table for part of the day. If you have small children, childcare might be wise. Luckily my children were old enough at the time that we could set up rules that worked pretty well for the three of us, although you'd likely want to check that with them.

I believe that the two greatest advantages of working from home are that first, you don't waste as much time in meetings as you do in an office and, second, your boss is far, far away.

If you're accustomed to working in an office, you probably don't realize how much time you've spent in meetings, both formal and informal (like when someone just stops by your desk, cubical or office). Social interaction is key and brainstorming can be productive, but it all takes up time. And all that time cuts into your productivity. Working from home gives you more time to do what you need to do to get your work done. I knew I'd gain my former commuting time but I didn't realize until I started how much additional time I'd find to report my stories and write.

The second benefit might sound funny but if like me, you tend to clash with your boss (witness my email mentioned earlier in this chapter) there's a definite benefit to not working in the same space as your boss.

My *PRWeek* editors were in New York, roughly 1,000 miles from me. When they made decisions I didn't agree with, I could simply lay down on my couch for a bit and let my anger pass. It's very difficult to quit in anger when you're working from home. You certainly can't storm out of the office. Where would you go? Do you storm out of your own house when you're the only one home?

My stint at *PRWeek* turned into the longest at any job in my career. I stayed until September 2005, almost seven years. During that time I worked for two publishers, three editors-in-chief and five managing editors. When I left I was the last of the original bureau chiefs (we had those titles even though no one else reported to us). Originally, there'd been someone in Boston, Washington and San Francisco, in addition to myself in Chicago. The Boston reporter left early on and that position was switched to Los Angeles. I was the exception to the rule at *PRWeek* by staying so long. In journalism such turnover is the norm, not the exception, except at the very highest levels.

But even at the top, rapid turnover is becoming more common. Witness what Bloomberg did when it bought *BusinessWeek* in 2009 – it fired almost everyone who was still there from my era, the 1980s, employees who'd given the magazine decades of service as insightful, top-flight journalists. Job security in journalism doesn't exist and I think the same is true for every other field today as the economy continues its transition. If you remember nothing else from this book, remember this: ***job security is a myth***. A company's loyalty to its workers is a myth. ***You are on your own so take care of yourself.*** In other words, always be job hunting.

Given how much I enjoyed working at home, why did I leave? My main reasons for being home, my children, were off to high school and college, and didn't really need me at home anymore. I missed social interaction, and I thought I missed being an editor, the one who made decisions rather than just carried them out. I also sensed that I'd overstayed my welcome and become too expensive for *PRWeek*. They'd rather hire another body in New York, whom they could more closely supervise, than try to keep tabs on me, 1,000 miles away. In short, it was just time to move on.

Besides, a journalist who covers one beat for a long time can get stale; it can be harder to find the real news because you develop a sense of having seen it all. I needed to write about something new. In light of the upheaval that's beset my profession in the first part of the twenty-first century I wonder why I ever longed to get back in an editor's chair. But first I needed to find a new job. How do you do this when you've worked at home for seven years? I pursued two paths at once, both of which, it turned out, nabbed me jobs.

Lessons for You:

✓ You need to take care of yourself, professionally and personally.

✓ Working at homes presents opportunities and challenges, be disciplined about it.

✓ Taking a step backwards, career-wise, can sometimes be a good thing.

Chapter 9

Re-Entering the Office World

The topic of how to re-enter the office world is more usually talked about in regard to women who have taken years off to raise their children and now need to find a way to reassert their worth to an employer.

Yet anyone who works from a home office, an increasingly common experience these days, also has much to prove when they seek to go back into an office setting. I first learned this in the 1980s after shutting down my home-based newsletter publishing business. An employer's lingering doubts about your sociability, your ability to follow orders and ability to be on time can all come up when you want to return to an office environment. These days, your technology IQ also is questioned. Did you keep up with new software, social media and other innovations while you worked at home?

Once I knew it was time to leave my home office, I decided to simultaneously try two ways to find an office job. The first was to create my own new job.

Search specialists often recommend this strategy. Job ads aren't where you find a new job, they argue. Instead, you need to identify a place where you'd love to work and then tell management what you can do for them, in other words, how you're ideal for a position they might not even have yet. This advice always sounded good but a bit far-fetched to me. But in July 2005, I saw a chance to do just that. I was still working for *PRWeek* and covering a conference held by a new specialized marketing trade association. The head of the group was a zealot on the topic of word of mouth marketing and, watching him speak, I could see people in the room were quickly becoming adherents. I felt his then-small organization was set for growth. So after his speech I approached him and asked if he'd started a publications department yet. He said no and I pitched the idea of how much income publications could bring to his new association. Since I'd worked at a trade association earlier in my career I knew an association's main sources of income are traditionally member dues, conference fees and publication advertising.

My pitch got his attention, and we agreed to discuss it in more detail. I'd started building the job I'd leave home for.

At the same time, though, I pursued a second path, and contacted friends to let them know I was job-hunting yet again. In other words, I networked. Recruiters and executive search types always stress networking, claiming that it's a highly effective path to finding a job, more effective than simply answering ads. As I've become more experienced in my field I've found networking is a more valuable tool. Quite simply, you need to build a network before you can network for jobs and that takes not only time but also proving that you're good at what you do. When you reach out to your network, they need to know they can recommend you without hesitation.

My networking involved reaching out to the person who had taken my old job – yes, at the company where I'd sent the angry e-mail. It had been sold since I'd left in 1998, the media giant that owned it had dropped it when it decided magazines were no longer where it wanted to spend its money. The banking and credit card magazines had a new owner and even new offices. The person who replaced me as editor had become editorial director of the group. When he and I met for breakfast, he mentioned he might be looking for someone if one of his editors retired as planned. I expressed my interest and we left it at that.

So by August of 2005, I had two lines in the water, while also answering ads, my old standby. Always be job hunting means continuously pursuing every possible job avenue. I was actively using three tactics to do so. I met again with the trade association head and became more excited about starting a publications department from scratch. We were trying to hammer out job terms as my daughter, my then girlfriend, now wife, and I flew to San Francisco on vacation. I recall being frustrated at not getting an e-mail offer while we were out there, freezing through typical late summer San Francisco days.

Finally, in early September the offer came through and I had my new job. My exact role was still to be determined and I quickly found out that I had one idea about my job duties while the association head had another. I wanted to take a conventional route: start a print magazine and supplement it with e-newsletters and Web news. He came from the world of technology start-ups and quickly explained to me he could realize a greater return on the association's limited financial resources from meetings, both real and virtual, than he could from a magazine. I had to admit his numbers made sense, something I used to think about when, a few years later, I worked at a more established trade association that was watching its publication advertising revenue disappear but also couldn't seem to make money from its meetings.

So if I wasn't going to publish a magazine, what would I do? He liked e-newsletters but again, our ideas on what they'd contain differed. I wanted newsletters filled with stories we wrote ourselves; he was happy with newsletters that aggregated content from other websites. Whether these items were timely or not didn't really matter since he didn't have news sense nor think he needed to get it. The e-newsletters weren't supposed to share news, but instead, to draw people to events and the association site and prove to its members that they were getting something for their dues. This was all going on in late 2005 and it really opened my eyes to the fact that the Internet and technology were radically changing my profession. Employing a journalist who's an expert on a given topic and letting him write about the topic isn't really important in the Internet age.

Customers crave constant information and at this point, calling it all 'content' and simply pushing it at them seems enough for most publishers. Publishers just want customer eyeballs on their online ads.

Advertisers pay publishers every time a reader clicks on, or through these ads and the more eyeballs, the more chance someone will click through. Today content – and I hate that term for its generic-ness – is simply words and pictures to run between the ads.

My boss also wanted a writer to put all the new specialized marketing principles that he'd been highlighting in speeches into white papers. My job involved days of following him around with a pad (which he laughed at since he walked around with a laptop) taking notes on everything he said to write up later. I told him he just needed a secretary, not a journalist. I knew this job I'd created was nothing like what I'd hoped it could be. I did get a great trip to New York out of my time there, staying at the Marriott in Times Square, probably the most expensive hotel room I've every had, but my time with the association amounted to about five weeks. Yes, five weeks. I tend not to list that job on my resume; it was too short a stint for even me to explain.

Luckily, my former co-worker came through with the editor's job we'd discussed and so I resigned from the trade group and I started at the magazine in October 2005. I stayed until 2007 when my friend, finally tired of dealing with superiors who didn't share his editorial vision, himself left for another job. Without him to shield me, I assumed I'd soon face staff cuts and work for someone who had less experience. Sure enough, I lost the competition to succeed my friend to a less-experienced editor and so moved on. I took a step back and became a managing editor at a trade association but after a year there, left to become editorial director at a third trade association. Both those jobs came from answering ads, by the way, so always be job hunting; I continually scan ads even when I'm not in the job market. You never know when a better situation might pop up.

These years working for trade associations, from late 2005 through June 2010, were a period when I looked for a job that I thought would be a safe harbor in tough times. Only a few months after taking the editorial director's job at the last association my publisher, who'd been there 10 years, was fired in a staff purge, leaving me reporting to a woman whose job it was to trim costs at all costs. She was essentially the Luca Brasi to the association president's Godfather. She allowed him to be the benign leader while she did the dirty work needed to keep the organization afloat during grueling financial times. She had no concept how to work with creative talent. Most of my two years working at that group were pure hell, mitigated only by the fact that the other journalists who worked for me were some of the best I'd ever worked with. Our great creative team produced some amazing work despite it all.

By mid-2010, I was done with the constant turmoil there and began job-hunting again. This time I responded to an ad that led me back to an old place of employment (which had been sold three times since I'd worked there in the mid-1990s). I started the job that I began at the beginning of this book. For a second time, I'd returned to an old place of employment which had a new owner. Do I advise going home again like that in your career? Did it work out for me? Well, not exactly.

Lessons for You:

✓ One way to find a new job is to convince an employer to create one for you. But beware, what you get may not be what you expected.

✓ A horrible boss can make even good working conditions seem horrible; run don't walk away from a horrible boss.

✓ Finding an agreeable work environment is worth a pay cut.

Chapter 10

The Late-Career End Game

If you're head's spinning as you try to keep up with all of my job changes, imagine how I feel. Writing this book and remembering all these changes is challenging, painful and just wonder-inspiring at times for me. All of the job searches, the disappointments, all the companies failing or being sold out from under its employees, all the friends who gave up on journalism and sought out new professions instead. It makes me weary, just remembering. But I've accomplished something far greater than the professional work I published and the teams I've led: I've survived. Thirty-five years is a long time to stay one step ahead of the unemployment reaper, yet this is exactly what I've managed to do.

My lesson for all of you who read this book is: (you should have this memorized by now) Always be job hunting. If you still hold onto it, banish the idea of job security from your head, your heart and your imagination. Be prepared to do what's best for you.

Yes, you absolutely owe an employer your full efforts and a good day's work. I'm not in any way advocating giving any less. Just remember that what you get in return for your efforts is a paycheck, not a guarantee of lifetime or even long-term employment. You may get promoted and you may even be one of the now rare employees who work for the same company for the majority, or even for all, of your career. I actually know someone, not in journalism but in manufacturing, who has done just this. He stayed even as the company went through a highly public bankruptcy. He moved from one city to another to stay employed by this same company. Frankly, I would've been bored at the same place all these years. But that's just me. I also know people who stayed at that first suburban chain where I worked all these years and still enjoy going to work every day. I wish them well.

Are you one of these types? If so, be sure that you know and practice what it takes to make you happy long-term in any given workplace. Is it a steady paycheck? Recognition as a star? The ability to stay in the background and not be called on for high-stress starring roles? Does creativity matter to you? How will you react when the company you work at runs into financial difficulties or makes major changes in its structure or, at a micro-level, in your job, your staff, your department?

These questions bring us full-circle, back to the job I'd just begun as I also began writing this book. A year and a half later, as I feared, not all has happened as I'd hoped. I was able to hire two staff writers but neither picked up on the intricacies of business writing. I even brought in a writing and business coach to help, but to no avail. So I let one go after a few months only to have my boss tell me that there'd be no replacement since ad sales were down. So now there were three, not four staffers reporting and writing for two magazines, Web sites, e-newsletters. I was doing two jobs and still longed to fire the other writer, but knew I couldn't. Then I'd be down to two people with no funds to replace him. This extra workload dragged down team productivity and my spirits.

On "The Apprentice," his reality television show, Donald Trump likes to say that losing in business is the worst, that it rips apart formerly happy, well-functioning teams, and prompts people to turn on each other in ugly ways. That's what's happened. Ad sales fell last year. The new publisher whom I'd hoped was a sales star is still trying to assemble an effective sales team. He's spent a great deal of time, (too much, in my opinion) looking into editorial matters because it's easier than finding and inspiring new sales people who can meet their quotas. His penchant for trying to hit sales home runs isn't working in the business we cover, one that's accustomed to slow, almost snail-like progress when there's any progress at all. His big-sell approach doesn't seem to be connecting with enough advertisers. He's not doing enough selling.

By the end of 2011, he'd decided to close one of my magazines and he decided this without consulting with me. We then fired the other under-performing employee. Instead of the closed magazine, I also was given responsibility for a second magazine, which the publisher acted as editorial director for, redesigning it with little editorial input. Despite his publisher title, in reality he's acting as this new magazine's editorial director while I'm serving as the managing editor, trying to get the one full-time staffer to dream up new story ideas and meet deadlines. I've known this staffer since 1996 when we worked together at another publication. Working with him again was one of the reasons I accepted my current job. Now, my publisher wants to fire him, and blames him for the lack of ads in the newly redesigned magazine he oversees. To blame an editor for a lack of ads is a bit like blaming someone walking with an umbrella for the fact that it is raining. I've refused to fire the editor and refused to interview people to replace him.

I'm wondering what will happen next. Will my friend be fired against my wishes? Will I be fired for being so insubordinate? Will the publisher be fired for not producing sufficient ad dollars for the two magazines? I doubt it will be the latter. The company likely will give him another full year to put up or shut up. Then, he'll be gone. I've worked for other owners who shuttled publishers in and out of a revolving door until they found one who could meet sales targets.

So maybe you can understand why I'm feeling weary. I really want to work for an employer who respects my talents, my experience and my read on how magazines function in today's multi-media world. And, oh yes, it would be nice if I don't have to pay for the sins of a sales staff that can't figure out how to convince advertisers that they still need magazine brands, which now include Web sites, social media, e-publications, conferences, Webinars and the like, to reach and be relevant to their customers.

I'm getting weary of selling myself to yet another employer and worrying about who'll want to interview a 58-year-old journalist? When I started out, everyone in my field seemed old. Now that I'm old, it seems all employers look for are low-cost people with 3-5 years' experience and no more. No one wants to pay me what I'd like to make with my experience.

So, how do I, or you if we're in the same boat, combat this weariness? It goes back to what I keep saying: Always be job hunting. Forget your age and bad work experiences and remember what you can offer a potential employer. Go into interviews, write cover letters and handle phone conversations with potential employers in an energetic, full-of-ideas mode. Remember why you love what you do and let that love shine through in every encounter. Keep updating your skills, either in your present job, or outside it if you have to.

I did the latter when I started a blog with a friend about a year and a half ago. I wanted to prove I could blog and also learn how search engines function and how they can drive visitors to a blog or a magazine's Web site. We finished 2011, our first full blogging year, with more than 100,000 visitors to our blog (guysandgoodhealth.com), pretty good for two amateurs, I think. Did I know anything about blogging when I started? No but I read everything I could find about it and then learned by doing.

I regularly do podcasts for work and have conducted video interviews. These aren't just part of my job. I also do this to prove to potential employers that I'm not just a print journalist which today is akin to being a covered wagon maker. I'm showing that I'm a multimedia journalist who also runs Facebook and LinkedIn groups. If you're an older journalist, join my LinkedIn group, "Journalists Over 40 Trying to Stay Relevant." I started it while at my last job where I wasn't able to do any Web work yet I still wanted the world to know that I was capable of it. Age isn't a barrier to anyone who wants to expand professional skills and abilities.

I thought the music had stopped for me in this chair, my last as a magazine editorial director. But a new career was just around the corner.

I've kept up to date on how companies use software to select certain resumes to review and I'm sending out cover letters these days that mimic the wording of ads in the hopes that will trigger the software that sends my resume up the decision chain. I'm also referring people to the recommendations I've gathered for viewing on my LinkedIn profile.

Don't just *tell* people you know about new technologies in your profession, *show* them. Do what a friend of mine who was laid off did. She went back to school to learn HTML and Web minutiae and is now doing work in that area.

I'm even considering walking away from journalism and utilizing my writing and communications skills in other fields. Switching to public relations at this point in my career isn't likely. I reached out to a former colleague who runs a major company's PR department to sound him out on a job and received a polite, "don't think about it" type of reply, not exactly encouraging. Career coaches say we should create new careers several times during our working life. Is this actually feasible, when so many people with greater experience are already out of work and hungry for whatever job comes along?

Honestly, there are times that I'm scared to death that the music has stopped in this game of musical chairs that's been my career. I'm not ready for early retirement and I certainly don't want to be forced into it. Part of me would love to stay home and start writing the plays I've talked about writing for the last few decades but the larger part of me thinks the time for that hasn't yet come. In addition some health problems mean I can't go without health insurance. Who can?

So if you were hoping this would end on an up-beat, rah-rah note, sorry. I'm a journalist, not a PR person. I've tried to give you ideas and approaches you can use to find your next job and the one after that. More important, I've reminded you that there's no job security and no one owes you a job. Finding a job is a battle, almost as big a battle as it is to keep one. But it's a battle you can win, or at the very least, fight on your own terms. Sometimes, at the end of the day, being able to say that can be pretty rah-rah in and of itself.

Lessons for You:

✓ Sometimes, survival is a victory in itself, rejoice in it.

✓ Career changing is becoming a way of work-life.

✓ We all get weary, take time to rest and then hit the job-hunting trail again.

Postscript:

Starting a New Career

Shortly after finishing a first draft of this book, I decided it was, indeed, time for me to leave journalism. I was frankly tired of working for bush-league publishers who don't value creative talent and, worse, haven't a clue how to make money in the internet age.

I became convinced of that decision when I went on a job interview in early 2012 to a publisher in suburban Chicago. All the men in the office were wearing ties in this age of casual dress. I asked the editorial director who was interviewing me what the story was. The owner, who comes by a few days a week, insists on it, he told me. The owner thinks men should wear ties, so everyone there wears ties. Now for all I know this owner is the best publisher ever, but he's also a quirky guy and I'm done with those, I don't have the patience for small-time publisher foibles like that anymore.

Even large publishers are struggling and they have no reason to hire someone like me who has been knocking around the minor leagues of journalism these past few years. I was like the Kevin Costner character in *Bull Durham*, it was time for me to hang up my spikes.

I took an inventory of what my skills are. I'm good at gathering and analyzing information. Complex situations don't faze me, they challenge me to figure them out. I love building teams. I believe passionately in the power of education to elevate children from impoverished neighborhoods into the white-collar world. I love writing about the food business because everyone can relate to it. The blog I write, guysandgoodhealth.com, is all about healthy eating, exercise and men's health, so food is a major part of it.

Me sitting in the last office I may ever have, circa early 2012. My new employer believes in open office floor plans, so I'm back in what looks an awful lot like an old-fashioned newsroom.

So I started answering ads for jobs where those skills and interests could help me. I wrote several non-profits advertising public relations jobs. I could never see myself as a front man for a profit-making corporation, but I could be a passionate advocate for a non-profit doing good works.

I applied for a PR job with two relatively new Jesuit high schools in Chicago that specialize in educating underprivileged children from some of the city's worst neighborhoods. I still believe no one could have done that school PR job better than me. I'm a product of Jesuit education myself, having attended Xavier High School in New York City. My high school changed my life, starting me on my journey from the blue collar world of my parents to the professional life I have led. Passion for that mission would have infused everything I did there.

Unfortunately for the schools, whoever was reviewing applications did not have the vision to even invite me in for an interview, likely because I did not have some pre-determined set of job credentials they thought they needed. That lack of out-of-the-box thinking disappointed me because it had been the Jesuits, an order of Catholic priests devoted to the power of education, that first taught me not only to think outside a box but to throw the box completely away.

Throwing the box away has led me to the job I now have, as a food industry analyst for a major international research firm. Rather than writing news stories, I will be writing and overseeing other people writing reports on the food and beverage industries. I am using many of the skills I have for this, but also learning an entirely new set of skills, tools, research techniques and corporate-speak.

I have to say it is the most frightening career move I have ever made. As I write this, I'm on a plane returning from a week of training for this new job at the company's London headquarters. I feel like a rookie just out of school. But I'm also invigorated to have such a completely new challenge.

And I hope it leaves you knowing you're never too old to try new career adventures. You too can throw that box of conformist thinking away and re-invent yourself. This book is only the beginning of our discussion on how you do that. I'll be continuing the discussion on the book's blog, alwaysbejob-hunting.com. Visit and enjoy the conversation.

John N. Frank
Evanston, Illinois
March 2012

Author's Notes

I started writing this book with the hope that the ups and downs I've experienced in my career could help others to find jobs they enjoy and also to weather travails in their job searching and in their careers.

If reading this has helped you, I'm glad. If not, come to alwaysbejobhunting.com and tell me what more I can do, this book is just the start of our discussion (and there's always the possibility of a second edition).

I started writing this book alone but it has turned into a family affair, which has made it all the more special for me. My daughter Jenny, an NYU graduate who is also an accomplished graphic designer, created the cover design for the book. If you need a designer, check out her work at jfranklyspeaking.com. I think she would be a great hire for you.

My son Matthew, an environmental designer, has contributed to the book's blog, writing about his own job hunting struggles when he graduated from the University of Minnesota in the very depths of the worst economic conditions the U.S. has seen since the Great Depression. I have no doubt he will make this world a better place environmentally as he moves forward in his career.

My wife Carolyn has been continually supportive, even though my job hopping sometimes keeps her up at night. She has brought light to my life in so many ways, it would take a massive tome to detail them all. Suffice it to say that she allows, and actively encourages, me to believe in myself. That was something I never had before in my life and it's a precious gift I constantly thank and love her for.

And I also have worked with extended family on the book. A dear, dear friend, Delia Flores, someone who jokingly calls herself the little sister I never wanted, agreed to be my editor.

Delia, a professional journalist and colleague from my Reuters days, did not just proofread my manuscript but acted as a true editor, calling me to explain things I hadn't explained, to leave out things that really didn't fit, to trim my run-on sentences, and to make better the sections that weren't holding true to the mission of the book.

She was there for many of the events in this book and so has seen me at my best and at my worst. We had lost touch for a few years but reconnected recently and I am so happy she's back in my life. Having her be a part of this is a reminder to me that things happen when they're supposed to in our careers and in our lives; I could not think of anyone I would have trusted more with the fruits of my labor.

Appendix

One of the usual questions I get when job interviewing is why I've worked at so many places in my career. My usual answer is that many of the places I worked no longer exist, often I saw the end coming and got out while I was still working rather than waiting until the place was sold or closed.

Here's the proof of that, a rundown of all my employers and their status, or lack of it, today.

June 1976 – December 1978
The Daily Herald
Arlington Heights, Ill.

My job: general assignment reporter, education reporter, business reporter

Still in business today, although dealing with all the challenges most newspapers face now. The editor today is someone who started shortly after I did. Indeed, this paper, owned by Paddock Publications, a family-run operation, has seen amazing editorial management longevity. The current publisher was managing editor when I worked there.

January 1979 – November 1979
Pickwick Papers
Park Ridge, Ill.
My job: Managing Editor of five weekly newspapers

Sold in late 1979 to another then Chicago suburban chain, Pioneer Press, papers in this group are now owned by the *Chicago Sun-Times* which itself has changed owners several times over the years trying to survive in today's brutal newspaper business climate.

December 1979 – February 1983
U.S. League of Savings & Loans
Chicago, Ill.
My job, assistant editor, associate editor, *Savings & Loan News*, a monthly magazine

A Chicago-based major trade association well known for its Washington clout in the 1970s and early 1980s, it eventually merged with another banking trade group as the savings and loan crisis of the 1980s led to the eliminations of hundreds of S& Ls across the country. By 1993, friends who had stayed at *Savings & Loan News* were unemployed.

February 1983 – October 1984
Reuters
Chicago Bureau
My job: Financial futures correspondent

Reuters, once owned by British newspapers, went public while I worked there and today is a subsidiary of Thomson Reuters, losing its independence in 2008. Still a major worldwide news service, probably one of the places I should have stayed. Left in an effort to save a marriage which ended anyway.

October 1984 – September 1987
BusinessWeek magazine
Chicago Bureau
My job: Financial markets correspondent

Now known as Bloomberg *BusinessWeek*, probably the most journalistically professional place I've worked. A large staff of reporters and editors across the U.S. and around the world made this the business magazine of record in the 1980s and 1990s. When revenues plunged by half in the late 2000s recession, parent company McGraw Hill sold it to Bloomberg LP for only $2 million plus debt assumptions.

Colleagues of mine, who had spent 20 years or more as correspondents there, were summarily fired by Bloomberg as it cut costs and redesigned the magazine. Another place I should have stayed but I left trying to save my failing marriage. If I had stayed, I likely would have been out of work in 2010 with other veteran staffers who now talk to each other in a special LinkedIn group.

September 1987 – March 1989
S.F. Communications
The Financial Futures Analyst newsletter
Evanston, Ill.
My job: co-founder and editor

A newsletter publishing company I started with a former Reuters colleague. We raised $110,000 in working capital, planning to do newsletters that provided analysis of the financial futures markets for savings & loans and other financial institutions hedging interest rate risk.

The stock market crash of 1987 happened shortly after we published our first issue. Our biggest investor then decided to pull out, demanding his money back, leading us to legal action that resulted in giving him half his initial investment.

Finding new investors proved impossible in the bad economy which followed the market crash. I took no salary for a year, doing freelancing and teaching to earn some money, while trying to sell bulk subscriptions to brokerage firms for their clients. When we shut down, we had no debt but only returned our investors, which included my mother, 10 cents on the dollar.

March 1989 – March 1990
Chicago Mercantile Exchange
Chicago, Ill.
My job: writer in the public affairs department

A job I took when I was unsure I still wanted to be a journalist, it quickly reminded me I was a journalist and so I couldn't wait to get out of this place. Spent a year and 10 days there and the only day my boss seemed happy with me was when I told her I was leaving; we had a great discussion on why I shouldn't work there.

March 1990 – April 1991
National Provisioner magazine
Chicago, Ill.
My job: Editor-in-chief

I took the editor's job as the company was planning to sell its real estate in a trendy part of Chicago to refinance its operations and rejuvenate its products. When the commercial real estate market collapsed, the sale fell through and the company was put up for sale. I left before the sale, assuming a new owner would want an editor of his choosing. My successor was indeed fired when the magazine was sold. Only one of the four editors I had worked with was kept when the deal was completed, but she would put me in contact with the new owner who I would work for on another magazine in 1993.

April 1991 – March 1993
Knight-Ridder Financial News
Chicago, Ill.
My job: Chicago Bureau Chief

Hired to clean out deadwood at the bureau, I oversaw 14 editors and writers, the largest group I've managed in my career. One of four major news services at the time covering financial markets, Knight-Ridder was fighting desperately to maintain its market share as Bloomberg, the then upstart news service, grew. The recession at the time was causing financial firms to scale back how many news services they purchased. I spent a good portion of my time here doing performance reviews and gathering data that people weren't meeting performance objectives, making it one of the most depressing jobs I've had.

In 1996, parent company Knight-Ridder put the news service up for sale. Knight-Ridder itself no longer exists, nor does the news service. Former employees chat in a Facebook group.

March 1993 – December 1995
Beverage Industry magazine
Northbrook, Ill.
My job: Editor-in-chief

This magazine was owned by Stagnito Publishing, which had bought the *National Provisioner*. I was able to hire a managing editor and an associate editor I'd worked with in the past here because Stagnito had bought the magazine and moved it from Cleveland, leaving the old staff behind.

I worked here when my divorce hit, owners and my boss were wonderfully understanding and supportive through some of the worst days in my life.

The company was growing but over-expanded and, by late 1995, had missed one paycheck during the summer to us and was shopping my magazine to raise money to keep the company afloat. We were told of a deal that November to sell us to someone who did a convenience store magazine in another

Chicago suburb. The owners there proposed I could stay if I took a 30 percent pay cut. I left. That deal fell through and in the following year the entire company was sold to an East Coast-based trade magazine publisher. It's been sold twice more since then.

January 1996 – December 1998
Thomson Financial
Chicago, Ill.
My job: Editor-in-chief and then associate publisher, editorial, *Card Technology* magazine

I was hired to start this magazine with no other full-time staff. Eventually I had four people reporting to me and oversaw the magazine, a newsletter, a series of directories and two trade shows. Left here after the head of our division fired someone who reported to me without letting me know about the plan. That boss of mine would leave to start his own publishing company. Thomson would sell off the division when it opted to get out of magazines entirely. Sourcemedia, which bought the group of magazine I worked in, has phased out *Card Technology* as a print product.

December 1998 – September 2005
PRWeek magazine
New York, N.Y.
My job: Chicago Bureau Chief

Left behind my management hat to become a reporter for this trade magazine that covers public relations. Through three editors-in-chief and five managing editors, this job was a sea of calm in my career, providing me the opportunity to hone my writing skills. But by 2005, I was getting the distinct impression that the then managing editor and editor thought I had overstayed my welcome. I also wanted to return to an office setting after having worked at home for so long.

September 2005
Word of Mouth Marketing Association
Chicago
My job: writer

I created this job, hoping to start and oversee a publications department for this just-starting trade group. I soon discovered the group's head thought I should follow him around taking notes on what he said to turn into white papers. Luckily, a colleague from my *Card Technology* days had become editorial director at Sourcemedia's Chicago office and was looking for an editor, so I quickly left. I was at WOMMA for such a short period of time I never put it on my resume.

September 2005 – June 2007
Sourcemedia

Chicago office
My job: Editor-in-chief of *Collections & Credit Risk* magazine

Really my return to the world of magazine management after working at home, I was having a great time here until the colleague who had hired me and served as my editorial director left to work with the old boss who had started his own publishing company after leaving Thomson. *Collections & Credit Risk* no longer exists as a print product either. Sourcemedia's answer to changing magazine economics has been to go digital, charging to access sites that cover a range of financial topics.

June 2007 – July 2008
National Association of Realtors
Chicago, Ill.
My job: Managing editor of *Realtor* magazine

I thought this would be fun since I'd written on and off about real estate throughout my career but I made a mistake taking a step backward, title-wise. Being a number two did not suit me, especially as signs of the massive U.S. real estate collapse began to surface and the organization went into denial. I'm the living embodiment of the saying "lead, follow or get out of the way." When I can't lead, I need to get out of the way, which is why I left here so quickly.

July 2008 – June 2010
American Marketing Association
Chicago, Ill.
My job: Editorial director

I took this job hoping to find the type of stability I knew at the U.S. League in its heyday. Unfortunately, days like that didn't exist for trade associations in the massive recession then engulfing the country. Not long after I started, my publisher was fired in a round of layoffs designed to cut costs. My new boss had no journalism management background and did not value what I was best at, putting out quality publications. I still miss the people who worked for me here, some of the most skilled professionals I've known. I helped one get another job after I'd left and she was ready to leave as well. Another has my old job there now. And the evil boss is gone, finally.

June 2010 – February 2012
BNP Media
Deerfield, Il. office
My job: Editorial Director, *PLBuyer* magazine, *Contract Manufacturing & Packaging* magazine, *Perishables Buyer* magazine.

This company now owns several of my past magazines, namely *Beverage Industry* and *National Provisioner*. Went here just as a new publisher came in to run the magazines for which I would be responsible. Hired new staffers but as I let go those who were not cutting it, I was not allowed to replace them, so by year-end 2011, I found myself doing three jobs while more are added on top of that. I decided during the holidays it was time to leave and likely time for me to end my journalism career. My publisher left a month after I did, failing to sell enough ads to keep the magazines healthy and unable to assemble a sales team that could successfully sell ads either.

February 2012 – present
Mintel International
Chicago office
My job: Category manager, food and drink

This job requires skills I developed as a journalist, such as editing, writing and trend following, but it also requires me to learn an entirely new set of skills, including statistical analysis I've never done at this level before. I go to work frightened every day, which is a good thing I think, it's keeping me alert and ready to learn.